Run! Run! Hitler's Coming!

HOW A YOUNG GERMAN GIRL ESCAPED THE HOLOCAUST

A TRUE STORY

IRENE GORDON ROSENTHAL

WITH
SHERRY ROSENTHAL

CO-AUTHOR'S FOREWORD

Like all Holocaust memoirs, my Aunt Irene Rosenthal's life story is unique and troubling, but ultimately hopeful.

Before this project I knew little about what my aunt endured before coming to America from Europe and in the early years after her family's arrival. Like many, perhaps most Holocaust survivors, she has always been more interested in getting on with life and savoring the present than in recollecting, much less dwelling on the past. That is a great strength of hers and one I have found typical of Holocaust survivors.

The story of her growing up, and of her adolescence and early adulthood has not been easy to come by for that reason. Understandably, Holocaust survivors are little given to looking back.

Irene Goldbaum (in America her father changed the family name to Gordon; then when she married my paternal uncle Dr. Sam Rosenthal she became Irene Rosenthal) was a born in Germany in 1926. Unlike many of her age and religion born there, she miraculously survived the Holocaust. This is the story of how.

Growing up myself in Southern California—back then a smaller, closer-knit place than now; whose sunny weather and coastal beauty offered many European post-World War II immigrants a new beginning; I was used to meeting Holocaust survivors. While none wanted their children, grandchildren and the rest of the world to ever forget the Holocaust, none including my aunt especially relished sharing their experiences of it.

There is a reason Holocaust memoirs take a long time to write. Like sufferers of nightmares that fade only uneasily once a new day breaks, few Holocaust survivors, including my aunt, cared to discuss what they had endured. When I was growing up, it was common for children and grandchildren and nieces and nephews to learn more of the Holocaust from books and films than their own relatives.

Questions about survivors' memories were generally off-limits. Those who summoned courage to ask were most often told "I don't want to talk about it." We, their children and grandchildren, their nieces and nephews, loved these tough and resilient if mysterious people and did not want to break their hearts. So, though fascinated and intensely curious, we did not pry into the sad, secret pasts of those dearest and closest to us.

But that about which someone cannot or will not speak becomes all the more fascinating to those inquiring.

And that in turn led survivors' children and others who wished to know and remember the truth to perhaps the greatest conundrum. How could we, their progeny keep the pledge asked of every *Bar* and *Bas Mitzvah* child and every Jewish confirmation teenager of the post World War II generation—to "never forget"?

A Holocaust memoir in the tradition of *Night* or *Survival in Auschwitz* or more recently *My Brother's Voice* is perhaps one of the best ways to "never forget" and assure that others do not. But these accounts are always, and only, uneasily produced. Any Holocaust memoir is first of all an enormous act of courage—the ripping open of past, only partly healed wounds so others might understand not just the person who survived but a unique and ignoble part of history. And every Holocaust memoir, though there are more now than when I was younger; perhaps because time has made writing them easier or at least possible if never easy, is a miracle of strength, endurance, bravery, and—yes—luck.

Before I began work on *Run! Run! Hitler's Coming* with my Aunt Irene I had always wanted to learn more about her early life. But the problem was one of what, when, and how to ask.

I knew from childhood that my aunt had survived the Holocaust. But her daughter Barbara - my first cousin - told me her mother did not like to talk about that part of her past. So I left the subject alone.

Then one evening in Santa Monica during a visit to my aunt and uncle; as the sun set its beautiful, uniquely California colors of pink and orange and lavender with a splash of red, and as we spoke of other things, my aunt offered to show me a draft of a memoir she had written, perhaps to show to her grandchildren, my second cousins Julie, Ian and Noah.

I read it greedily in about an hour and when I finished I told her I thought, having recently co-authored *My Brother's Voice*, that it should be made public. As a past *Bas Mitzvah* girl and confirmation teenager who'd promised to "never forget"; I confess I was more eager for its publication than she. But this is how our collaboration began.

As I had long suspected, my aunt's early life proved fascinating. She was well known as the most brilliant member of our family when I was growing up—even long before she attended law school and subsequently became a well regarded attorney and judge.

I knew she was German by birth but somehow she had never seemed foreign born, like so many other immigrants I knew. She spoke pure American English, slang and all—with only the faintest trace of an accent. She was always completely at ease in the Southern California milieu of the 1960's and 70's in which I (and her children, my first cousins Michael and Barbara) grew up. Later I came to understand that this is a quality shared by Holocaust survivors—adaptability.

My aunt and I also had a personal connection that included certain core values and interests. For example she alone seemed to understand my thirst for knowledge and higher education. Other family members were mystified, annoyed; even hostile when I decided to pursue a Ph.D. What was that, they wondered. Who needed it? Where would it lead? But my Aunt Irene understood.

Years later I learned she had experienced something similar when she decided in her late thirties with two grown children, to attend law school and pursue her long cherished dream of becoming an attorney and judge.

Nowadays such decisions are more common among women; in the mid 1960's however they were exceedingly rare and took enormous courage. Today I understand more about where that courage came from and just how early, painfully so, my aunt's courageous core was formed.

Other benefits of her courageousness have accrued to our family. My Aunt Irene provided me an early example of the importance to one's own happiness and fulfillment of following one's heart and mind, in pursuing a career and in other endeavors. This story is about that, too.

Sherry Rosenthal
Las Vegas, Nevada
April 2013

CONTENTS

PREFACE

As I write this from Santa Monica, California overlooking the beautiful Pacific Ocean, long past and far away from a childhood spent running from Hitler—within Germany, then on to Holland, to Italy and eventually the United States—it seems almost another lifetime ago. In terms of how my world has changed it *was* another lifetime ago—spent with my parents and my younger sister Susi and other close relatives moving from country to country, our wealth gone, sometimes just a step ahead of the Nazis. We were a family of once-prosperous German Jews fleeing for our lives.

But it is just one lifetime—mine—and though time and the happiness of my adulthood in America have soothed much of the pain, some of the *angst* of a childhood spent in exile stays with me even now.

I am alive and well; healthy and happy—a rare blessing for German Jews born in 1926—but I am still scarred by it all, if no longer scared by any of it.

My story is distinct from most Holocaust stories. It is, perhaps more than anything, a validation of my parents' brave decision to leave Germany and all we had there so my younger sister and I might have a new chance at life however hard and uncertain that life might be.

In that sense this memoir is about the importance of life and how that transcends comfort and the quest for personal possessions—something I consider too important to many Americans these days.

My family had material wealth in abundance before Hitler came to power but we had to leave it all and start again from scratch. And then we had to keep moving. For a long time no country wanted us. Only the United States wanted us for keeps.

Why write all this now, in my eighties? Maybe it is because I want to leave a record, some personal account. Maybe it is because something of where I have been and what I have experienced might interest or even benefit my grandchildren's generation.

I think I also waited so long to write this story because there are so many other Holocaust stories already written—famous ones and obscure ones alike—many more heart-wrenching than mine. But maybe my particular story of loss, regeneration, and the faith to carry on toward a better tomorrow is something whose time has come in 21st century, post-recession America.

CHAPTER ONE

BORN LUCKY

Mine is not the usual Holocaust story: my family neither survived Hitler's concentration camps nor fled to the woods, like most Nazi survivors in Germany where I was born and in many other areas of World War II Europe. Mine is a whole different kind of story about a wealthy girl born into secure circumstances who saw it all come apart beginning at age six, courtesy of Hitler and the Nazis, and whose parents had to start again—in their fifties, their wealth gone—in America.

We were the lucky ones among family and friends; we at least survived to tell the tale.

Two separate but related pieces of luck spared me the fate of many German Jews during World War II. First my father was prescient enough to know from early experience that anti-Semitism ran deep in Germany and that Hitler would plow it even deeper.

He knew long before Hitler came to power that Germany could and would turn against the Jews that lived there—assimilated or not. One particular experience my father had in the German Army during World War I, long before I was born, taught him that.

As a young soldier my father had seen his best friend, another Jewish soldier, be shot and die for Germany. As my father's best friend lay dead and still bleeding a German officer came over, kicked the dead body and declared, "Good, there's another Jew dead."

Later, before leaving the army to begin his business career, my father avenged this horrific act against a friend he had loved like a brother. But after that fateful day my father never again felt comfortable in his homeland, even if for some time, until he left the army himself, he continued to lay down his life for it.

From that day on my father would have been prepared to abandon Germany on a moment's notice. And once we left he never looked back, at least not seriously, since in his mind he had been preparing to leave for a very long time.

I must be clear however—my father loved Germany and the German way of life. He came from a family of assimilated Jews and had friends from all walks of life. Germany was his home—as much as it was, or had ever been, the home of any stiff-armed "*Heil Hitler*" saluting Nazi—maybe even more so; since Germany had for generations been very good to my father's family. But to his credit, and for our sake, he was able to make the cold-blooded decision to leave when that became necessary for our survival.

That does not mean that it didn't break my father's heart to leave Germany; despite his later success in America he was never again as happy as when we had all lived together in Germany, my aunt, uncle, cousins, grandmother and the four of us, all in one huge roomy house before Hitler took over. But my father's unsentimental willingness to leave his homeland and all he had achieved there was my first piece of good luck.

My second piece of good luck was that my family had the money to buy our way out due to my father's and my uncle's hard-earned prosperity at our family jewelry business.

My father's name was Max Goldbaum. Later in San Francisco where we settled permanently he became Max Gordon, an easier name in America. After all my family had endured in Europe, once we got to America it was all about blending in, and my father thought a name change would help us blend in. It probably did, and so in America I was known as Irene Gordon, not Irene Goldbaum—another part of Germany left behind. Later when I married I became Irene Rosenthal.

I have now been Irene Rosenthal for over 60 years, but before that I seemed to shed last names the way I shed possessions as we journeyed from place to place. At the same time this taught me, early on, who I am inside. Who you are inside has nothing to do with either what people call you or what you own.

So my two pieces of good luck, first my father's intuition about Germany's dangerous level of anti-Semitism; and second, my family's wealth, made all the difference for our survival. Without such luck I would have perished at Auschwitz in nearby neighboring Poland or in another of Hitler's many death camps throughout Europe. My Jewish school friends whose families stayed in Germany did not survive.

Still I paid a price. Everyone in my family paid a price, including, perhaps especially, my younger sister Susi and me. Our childhood simply stopped in any normal sense. From age six I had no familiar surroundings, no normal school years, and no steady friends, acquaintances, or country to call my own.

Actually, I had a lot of countries—first Germany, next Holland, then after that, for a longer time, Italy. But after Germany none of them ever felt like *my* country; and we were never in any of them long enough to truly make it so.

Then there was America at last. America became my country. But by then childhood was over and had been for a long time.

Before that however Pforzheim, Germany as I remember it (before the Nazis took over) was a very nice place to live. In Pforzheim my sister and I had what other children had—friends and school and dolls. We always wore pretty clothes. We had the best toys. Of course I didn't understand the concept of wealth back then; no child does at that age. But even so I knew that I was surrounded by the nicest things and that not all children my age had as much as my sister and me and our cousins (my uncle Erwin and Aunt Ilse's children) Walter and Annie.

Very often though with something good (I learned early) there can be a bad side to it; and the bad side to being a wealthy child is that she has more to lose than a poor child. And I lost a lot.

When we left Germany I had to leave my toys, dolls, books, the treasures of childhood. After that I was never attached to possessions, even once we moved to America, the land of plenty.

In America I soon learned how everyone wants lots of possessions—the more, and the more expensive, the better, or so many believe. But I stopped thinking that way when I was six years old and had to leave my precious belongings in Germany. And I'm sure that is why I have never wanted grown-up "toys", cars, boats, jewelry and the like, the way many Americans do. I learned early on in Europe how easily, how arbitrarily, all can be taken away.

I also learned back then what *cannot* be taken away. No one can take away the person you are. No one can take what you know, your education, things you've studied, read and learned. And you can add to your education wherever you are, inside and outside a classroom.

I have learned something everywhere I have lived, though I have preferred some places to others. Most importantly no one can take away your core values.

But objects can be taken and often are in the most surprising ways. For example who would have believed when I was a first grader playing happily with my sister Susi and our cousins Walter and Annie, we privileged four, that everything our family had worked for would be lost before I turned seven?

But that happened.

CHAPTER TWO

THE WEIGHT OF BEING GERMAN

Affter Hitler seized power Germany turned into a death trap for Jews, although many Jewish people were slower than others to realize this and millions of others never did. That is where my good luck with my father's unsentimental view of Germany especially comes in.

Against this increasingly dangerous political backdrop my family finally fled Germany for good in 1937, just a brief while before it would have been too late to get out. For Jews who did not take the danger seriously, it was a fatal mistake. One might say looking back—and it wouldn't be overly dramatic—that I was born into extreme danger, since in Germany in the mid-1920s the anti-Semitism that would force my family out was already heating up, fast.

Still, I was born in *pre*-Nazi Germany; and for my first few years, even with the conspicuously Jewish name of Goldbaum, life felt normal to me. I have no doubt looking back that my father and my uncle Erwin who ran our family business were experiencing daily anti-Semitism even then. But I was too young to understand that.

Anti-Semitism or any prejudice does not just spring up fully formed; it builds quietly for years, decades, even centuries. That was the case in Germany. Our family's ability to live peacefully, productively and without personal danger in Germany as we had done for generations ceased once Hitler came to power. But before then anti-Semitism in Germany was not strong enough to discourage our living there or to hold us back from success.

As the 1920's turned into the 1930's however it became clear to my parents and my Aunt Ilse and Uncle Erwin, who shared our house that we all had to leave.

Other German Jewish families, unable to contemplate the huge potential loss of livelihood, friends and all else they knew turned a deaf ear to the increasing roar of anti-Semitism. For that they, including some of my German school friends and their families, paid with their lives.

❈

Nowadays the fear and agony of those early times seems almost unreal, like torn-out pages from German storybooks almost a century old; or blurry smoked-up scenes from Peter Lorre films or other much-dated movies of that time. But when I close my eyes and really think back, I still feel the terrifying realness of it all—the panic that leapt regularly into my throat; or the tightness in my chest, or the sensation of a heavy dropped ball in the pit of my stomach. That was what it felt like simply to live as a Jew in Germany back then, and perhaps even more so as a small child unable to comprehend what was truly happening.

In childhood once you know there is a reason to be sad, sadness sets in, along with vigilance. And so it did with me. I still remember the vigilant sadness. I would not have believed back then that I could ever be happy again. Where could we go now that we could all still be together—my parents, grandmother, aunt, uncle and cousins, all in the same house, the way we had lived since I was born?

❈

In America the weight of being German and Jewish eventually got lighter; although even to this day it has never completely lifted off me. Some of my happiest times have included my college years at the University of California at Berkeley, where I met my future husband Sam. And university life, where I could finally exercise my mind to the fullest, was pure heaven for me.

But my deepest happiness, of a depth that would have been unfathomable to me in my youth, has been our long marriage of over 60 years, our children Michael and Barbara, and our three grandchildren, Julie, Ian and Noah. In my youth spent on the run, I could not have imagined that the world could or ever would give me such joy.

I have also been lucky enough to have a fulfilling career that has suited me, first as a lawyer and later a judge. After our children had left for college I applied for and was accepted to law school, a long cherished dream I'd put on hold while Michael and Barbara were growing up.

I think now that I was born to be a lawyer. Even back in Germany as a child, before I could possibly have known what lawyers did, I yearned to become one someday, and from there to become a judge. I have always loved working with language and ideas; and I especially enjoy the writing process and the clear thought it takes for good results. And I am a natural skeptic and perhaps a bit of a cynic—traits honed during my rootless years that turned out to serve me well professionally.

I also like thinking, generally. I appreciate that thinking is hard work for many, but there is something almost recreational in it for me. I excel at the objective-yet-skeptical kind of thinking that is important for lawyers and judges. To be sure there are other important ways of thinking but the lawyer/judge way is my particular gift.

My analytical self is perhaps the German in me coming through. Thinking and analysis of the careful, detailed, kind that comes naturally to me are often considered "German traits". Many Germans, Jews and non-Jews alike, have tended to excel at such thinking. Some of the world's best thinkers including Freud, Marx, Einstein, Hannah Arendt and others have been German or Austrian Jews.

German education (which is not pleasant) stresses clear, careful thinking. However there are also plenty of non-Germans who are equally good thinkers, including many friends and colleagues I have known in America and elsewhere. So thinking is not a purely German trait even though thinking well is emphasized and rewarded in German culture.

German people are also known for hard work and I have always been a hard worker. But I know many hard workers who are not German including my husband, whose background is Lithuanian. Other stereotypic German traits have to do with being stubborn and rigid, and although I am neither, I have had people assume that I am both just because I am German.

❖

I did not ask to be born German or Jewish, in the same way someone else would not ask to be born Chinese, African, Argentine or Russian. You are born as who you are and you make the most of it, or try to. Even now I have an odd, uneasy relationship to my German roots because after all Germany did not want my family since we were Jews. But my roots *are* German and like all Germans I have benefitted from the good stereotypes and suffered from the bad ones.

On its own being German is neither good nor bad, although especially around the time of World War II it was considered bad. But not all Germans were Nazis, either—a stereotype of non-Jewish Germans that lingers from the World War II era. Living in so many countries at an early age taught me there are good people (and not so good ones) of all nationalities and backgrounds, including Germans, Jews, Italians, Dutch, and many others. What matters is who you are inside; and you take that with you wherever you go.

CHAPTER THREE

MY AMERICAN SELF

A person's 'self' is a combination of things—heredity; genetics; early childhood experience; school; peer influences, etc. Recently when visiting one of my regular doctors - to confirm that all my still-mysterious invisible parts are yet in proper order and functioning well, we discussed recording our lives for our children and grandchildren.

He told me:"My parents took some of the very first videos of us when we were children. We now look at them, not so much to look at ourselves but to catch glimpses of our parents who are hardly ever on the screen and we can seldom find even a glimpse of them."

In writing this I am recording memories of my parents and relatives their age and older, not on videos obviously, but in words. And I am recording memories of my own life - how I survived to become an adult in America and what I did with a life that through sheer luck was not snuffed out.

I believe my difficult German girlhood helped give me the stamina to go to law school and then work as a lawyer and a judge at a time when I was no longer young, and when it still went against the grain for women to be lawyers or judges.

I studied law and took the California Bar Exam at a time when the numbers of women even studying law, much less passing the bar and going to work as lawyers, was much smaller than today. Jews in particular are often criticized more than praised for wanting to be lawyers, judges, doctors, dentists, or other types of professionals. The stereotype (the German stereotype is a compliment to Germans; but an insult to Jews—always a confusing conflict for me) is that Jews simply want to make lots of money.

Yes, this is sometimes true of Jews, but it is also true of other groups. I cannot think of any group without at least some members who wish to make a lot of money. It is simply human nature to want to do well financially.

But there are also many Jews throughout history who have devoted themselves to art, research, scholarship, and other things that do not necessarily lead to making lots of money. So to say that Jews want only to be rich is as inaccurate as saying that Peruvians or Greenlanders want only to be rich. Granted, just about anyone would rather be rich than poor and most would choose wealth over being middle class. But contrary to stereotype, becoming rich is not the driving force of Jews as a group, just as that is not the driving force of any group.

I did not seek to become wealthy through my work as a lawyer and judge —I simply liked the work and found myself to be naturally good at it. I do know some Jews who are interested mainly in making lots of money as an end in itself, but I also know far more who might like to make lots of money if that were to happen, but still don't have that as a main goal.

My own reasons for wanting to be a lawyer and judge never had to do with money. I just thought these jobs would be interesting, challenging, and mentally stimulating for me, and that I would enjoy the work and probably be good at it. I hoped to contribute something to my community. It was never about the money.

❧

Instead, my husband Sam and I are both curious about the world, other people, and how things work. We have done a lot of traveling that we have enjoyed. Our curiosity extends naturally to other people. We share many good long-term friends. We have a wide circle, not because we seek out anyone in particular, but because we and our various friends have a lot of shared interests.

We both read a lot and we are always finding new reading materials—novels, the classics, non-fiction books. Our other interests tend toward classical music, golf, and art. We also love to play bridge.

If I were to identify a third piece of good luck it would be my marriage.

I had the good fortune to find a husband (he is not German) who is a lot like me in his tastes and interests.

Today I feel American heart and soul; I speak, think, dress and act American. I dream in American English. The happiest part of my life is the *American* part. Even now I am still integrating all the other parts.

Still in America I have found it difficult at times to catch a real glimpse of myself—of who I was before and after leaving Europe and who I am today. At first I was too busy, too preoccupied with husband, family, work and getting on with life. The easiest way for immigrants to manage is to not look back much. But one can also forget, then, all that makes a self.

And at other times I've doubted there was even a real self to see. The task of knowing oneself is, I believe, doubly hard for immigrants since there is the self you were in the old country and the one you are here, and they *are* different; they must be different. The real work of being an immigrant is to integrate the selves.

Therefore even in my eighties I am a work-in-progress. Perhaps that is simply the case for any who shed their original identities and assimilate new ones, like second skins. These newer skins never fit quite right. Eventually they become wearable though; like a too-big shoe a growing foot expands to fill.

CHAPTER FOUR

BEFORE HITLER

Our house in Pforzheim, a city in Southwestern Germany on the rim of the Black Forest, sat majestically at the outskirts of the town. It was a very large house, with many rooms on the first floor which constituted our quarters. The second floor, whose layout was a duplicate of the first, was where Aunt Ilse, Uncle Erwin and our cousins Walter and Annie lived. An unusual thing about our family was that my mother and my Aunt Ilse were sisters and my father and my Uncle Erwin were brothers. So when my cousins Walter and Ann were born to Aunt Ilse and Uncle Erwin, I had two first cousins on both sides.

My grandmother on my father's side also had her own spacious apartment on the third floor of our house. A wide beautiful staircase connected us all. Therefore I was born into a family that was unusually close, physically and otherwise. But within a few years fate would spread us far and wide.

Our house had been built by my father and Uncle Erwin. A friend of Erwin's had been the architect. Whenever this friend was referred to though, it was never in connection with the design of the house. No, he was remembered because his leg was run over by a streetcar. I often pictured this in my child's mind-the outstretched leg under the moving car.

I recall our huge house especially in the springtime, the last of the winter snow having melted, and with the air being cold and crisp. The dogs would bark whenever the house was approached. We had two dogs, Herta, a large female German shepherd, and Zinga, a large female black poodle. Together they guarded the house.

The Lindbergh kidnapping had frightened my family, thus the acquisition of these two huge guard dogs (which I recall as not being very friendly) to warn of any approaching strangers.

The house was the center of my existence in these early years. To this day I remember the address: *Gravelotte Strasse 13*. The house still stands today, in Pforzheim. The last I heard, it had been turned into a huge doctors' office building. Pforzheim was bombed by the Allies in 1945, but since our house was located on the outskirts of the city it was not damaged in the bombing.

My parents drilled our street address into my memory. We moved into the house in 1927 or 1928. We left in 1932, when I was six. I lived for four or five years in it, not a very long time but most of my vivid early memories are bound up within it.

Our house had been built on a quiet, wide street surrounded by an enormous garden of several acres. The stone steps that led up from the street were flanked on each side by a number of plants, of which I remember only one called bleeding hearts.

There were also rhododendrons that grew beneath the front windows with huge showy blossoms; and pink and blue hydrangeas, my grandmother's favorites but too stiff to the touch for me; and colorful lilacs on the southern side where our rooms were located.

In the back was an enormous sand box surrounded by currant bushes and trellised grapes that never ripened in the cool climate. On the north side of the house was an asphalt road lined with apple and cherry trees. This led in turn to a side road that made a service entrance.

In the very back of the property we grew cucumbers, tomatoes, carrots, rhubarb, and lettuce. That area also had a large compost heap which was great for jumping on but also frightening because we could feel the heat in it.

I remember rabbits in a hutch one year and puppies nursed carefully by Herta the German shepherd that same year. When I was given one to hold I accidentally dropped it and felt dreadfully upset about that for a long time.

Pforzheim's winters were bitterly cold. We had skis and practiced on the snow covered front lawn which sloped toward the street. Bundled in heavy wool clothing that inevitably became wet, I remember all this as being difficult chilling work rather than fun. But my sister and I learned to ski at an early age and we even had our very own "bunny slope" right outside the house!

Ice skating was different and much more fun. Each winter my mother, an avid tennis player, took us to the tennis club to which she belonged. The tennis courts would be flooded with water, making the whole area into a skating rink. Lights were strung around the court, since the daylight hours were short. Music was piped in with a gramophone.

There would be refreshments of hot chocolate, cakes, coffee, and I'm sure other stronger beverages not suitable for children. I loved skating, listening to the music, and watching the other skaters in colorful costumes.

Still, generally in the winter I had a perpetual cold. My nose ran all the time and I was forever looking for a dry handkerchief. Kleenex had not yet arrived and plastic was not available back then to keep clothing waterproof.

As glad as I always was to come inside from playing in the snow, this was nevertheless a painful experience. My nose, ears, and hands thawed out slowly and would be aching and red.

During those winter months especially, I preferred playing in the house. In the cellar there were long wooden slats where the apples, turnips, rutabagas, carrots and beets were stored. The smell of the cellar was tart and strong. There was also a bin with potatoes and a great many cabbages.

Most of all I liked the smell of the coffee beans. My father and his brother had a customer in South America who sent them fresh coffee. It was then roasted in Pforzheim and stored in large bags in the cellar. In the mornings it was my task, as soon as I was old enough, to put the coffee in a coffee mill and grind it by hand.

Breakfast back then consisted of coffee with a lot of warm milk for me and less warm milk for the adults. Cream of wheat or oatmeal was on the breakfast menu for us as children. We were required to finish the portion served to us, something that left me with an intense dislike of oatmeal all my life.

Some of my fonder recollections are of various outings we took. I loved going places. Early on it was to a farm in back of the house to feed the chickens, clutching the remains of my morning's bread. Later on it was with my much loved Aunt Tala, short for Natalie, down the hill to a bakery to feast on hot chocolate and a chocolate covered cream puff filled with whipped cream. That tasted especially delicious on a chilly day after a long walk!

Or my father would take me with him to his factory where I could sit in his glass enclosed office, looking at everyone working and trying to sit quietly. The factory had a busy, serious atmosphere that awed me. The foreman known to me as Herr Boger, treated me courteously but I felt myself to be a distraction and out of place. There were tiny glass enclosed scales to weigh diamonds, drawings for future designs, complicated mechanical tools, none suited to an active lively little girl who disliked sitting still.

And the family jewelry business was nothing if not serious. My father and uncle together with my aunt Tala, their sister, had sold jewelry door to door after the end of the First World War. With their savings they had opened the factory. They were granted a license to buy gold for it and during the terrible inflationary times in Germany they became successful.

They worked very hard. My uncle and my father left the house together by 7 a.m. and came back at 7 p.m. They came home at noon for the midday meal and returned to work by 1 or 2 p.m. six days a week.

My memories of my father during those years include watching him shave in the mornings, sharing meals where table manners were scrupulously observed, and of Sundays when friends and family dropped by for our usual Sunday afternoon *Kaffeklatch*.

CHAPTER FIVE

SUNDAY *KAFFEEKLATCH*

The Sunday afternoons I recall most vividly were in summer. For these we had an enormous round table set in the garden at the back of the house. Since my father and his brother Erwin had become successful businessmen, our garden was the hub of the family.

My paternal grandmother was bursting with pride at her children's success and she in particular loved to hold court there. Both of her sons, my father and my uncle Erwin, and her daughter my aunt Tala adored her. My grandmother was a handsome woman with a stately, erect carriage, even into her eighties. She had a beautiful head of white hair, arranged in the popular Gibson Girl fashion of the time. Typically she wore black with a touch of lilac or soft rose to set off her lovely skin and blue grey eyes.

One of my great delights was pulling the strings of her corset in the mornings. She smelled of talcum powder and eau de cologne and always wanted me to pull just a little tighter. Even as an old woman she took great pride in her figure, which was still good.

She had beautiful teeth that she kept in a glass at her bedside table and she refused to let me come in to visit until she had put them into her mouth. She loved to cook and liked to make hot chocolate for me.

But she no longer baked on Sundays, as she once had. Cataracts had caused her vision to dim and two surgeries had not improved it. So my mother and my aunts provided the *kaffeeklatch* food, which was regional.

I remember huge onion pies, more like tarts than Quiche Lorraine, and a cake made with pumpernickel flour and filled with dark juicy cherries. None of it was sweet and none was to my liking.

There was also lots of hot coffee served with hot milk or with whipped cream. My aunt Tala alone inevitably included something I liked: cookies, a cream puff covered with chocolate, or some candy. This was strongly against my mother's orders. Sugar led to tooth decay.

Along with Aunt Tala would be her husband Sepp (short for Joseph) and their beloved Dachshund, Waldis, whose high pitched barking and jealous ways I found annoying. Tala wore glasses and was not considered good looking but I loved her more than anyone. There was a sweet presence about her like a perfume that enveloped you with a loving kindness far stronger than mere beauty.

Her voice sounded like a caress and the moment I heard it I flew toward it. But Tala's early life had not been a charmed one. She had had a sad romance with a young man killed in the First World War. He was a Catholic, she was Jewish and intermarriage in those days was forbidden by my grandmother. My father and my uncle then chose Sepp for her.

Sepp was a watchmaker, a dapper man with salt and pepper hair and a bristly salt and pepper moustache to match, carefully trimmed but always with a smell of stale cigars on it. Tala and Sepp were devoted to each other and to Waldis. Many years later I learned that Sepp had been ill with syphilis and although he was cured of the disease, that had caused my aunt to have three miscarriages and a stillborn baby. This sad part of her life may have been why my sister and I and our cousins were especially dear to her.

There were other aunts and uncles around on those Sunday afternoons as well, including my aunts Blumchen, Rose, Mathilde and their husbands. I remember them mostly because of the gifts they brought me, including beautiful dolls with real hair and lovely handmade dresses.

There would be doll furniture and handmade pillows and blankets for my doll carriage; a silver soup spoon, engraved with my name, Irene; a children's fork, knife and spoon set together with a *schieber* (pusher) to push the food onto the fork. Back then in pre-war Germany, being a child often meant playing at being an adult; and children's toys, beautiful and special though they were, reflected that.

CHAPTER SIX

VISITS TO HAMBURG

When my mother and father married, according to my mother, she had a written agreement with him that she could visit her family in Hamburg twice a year. After I was born I too visited. Hamburg was damp and cold and I remember a great deal of rain always falling there.

My earliest memories of my maternal grandmother's house were of the chickens. She kept little chickens in the back yard that had feathered legs that resembled little pantaloons. I fed them occasionally and was allowed to gather the very small eggs.

Chickens were an especially important food source to many older Germans back then. After the First World War and the terrible difficulty of getting enough to eat, keeping chickens and having fresh eggs represented security.

In Pforzheim, too, I had a great aunt Auguste who always offered us an egg when we visited. Such offerings were common. This was long before worries about cholesterol surfaced, and in those days fear of hunger loomed large among all who had survived the First World War.

My grandmother Adele, my maternal grandmother, whom I called Omi, was a powerful figure in my childhood. She had borne six children. Her oldest had died after being immunized for smallpox. Five children survived: my uncles, Ernst, Gerhardt, Werner, my mother's sister Ilse, and finally, my mother.

My maternal grandmother's house was very large and comfortable in a Victorian fashion. My most vivid memories are of a huge dining room with potted plants that my sister used to dispose of unwanted food, especially liver, while the grownups were involved in solemn and frequently heated debates on some adult topic or other.

There were Persian rugs, a grand piano in the library, a large staircase in the middle of the house and books, books, books. I was not allowed in the kitchen or in some of the other rooms.

My Omi was strict. Her husband had died when my mother was seven or eight years old, and after that Omi had reared her entire brood alone.

My uncle Ernst was the oldest. The family had Sephardic origins. Their hair was dark. My mother's hair was as black as ebony and soft, whereas my Aunt Ilse's was black and Oriental in texture. Their skin was olive-toned. They were all short in stature. Ernst my oldest uncle was typical - short, dark skinned, brown eyed. He had a large nose and a wicked sense of humor.

In order to avoid the army, Ernst had gone to Bolivia to work on a sugar plantation. While there, he'd begun living with a local woman of color. When my grandmother heard about this union, she ordered him home. He returned. He was found to be too flatfooted for the army and lacked intellectual skills to enable him to make a living in postwar Germany. So my grandmother bought him two apartment houses in New York. He had excellent mechanical skills and maintained them well. He lived on the rents, although he was very soft hearted toward his tenants when they had difficulties, especially if they were female.

My second uncle Gerhardt had married a woman named Erika and fathered two children, Gisela and Alfred. Gerhardt was a lawyer. By the time I met him, he was a very quiet man, not given to interaction with me. He had been gassed in the First World War and that had left him both physically and psychologically weak.

My favorite of the three uncles on my mother's side was Werner. He was interested in me, perhaps because I was the first of the children in the family, or perhaps because we shared certain traits. He appreciated my endless curiosity and tried to answer my questions with patience and understanding. He also enjoyed sharing books with me. He had a quiet sense of humor and often teased me. Like his older brothers Werner was a short and slight man. His voice was soft and a bit wheezy and asthmatic sounding. And like his older brother Gerhardt he was a lawyer, if a more gregarious one.

I was intensely interested in Uncle Werner's beautiful woman friend, Marianne. She was by far the most glamorous of all the figures in my childhood. We played games in which she figured as the desirable and the romantic fantasy figure dressed in a fabulous wardrobe. (My sister inevitably was the one to play the role of Marianne). Uncle Werner traveled to Italy during my early years and sent me hand embroidered dresses that reflected his excellent taste. He also composed a poem teasing me about my vanity.

Books were another of his favorite gifts to me and the ones he chose for me were invariably interesting, no mean feat considering the age disparity between us. He always seemed to know what I would like to read.

Many years later after I was married and Werner had wed Marianne after her husband's death and we had not seen each other for several decades I visited him and he asked me after the cursory small talk, "What books have you been reading?" He knew even after all that time and distance exactly how to catch up on our relationship!

My aunt Ilse, my mother's sister and also my father's brother Erwin's wife, was a painter. A highly intelligent, artistic woman she was striking to look at with her jet black hair pinned up with a comb. She took singing lessons in my early years and I recall *Santa Lucia*, sung in Italian wafting through the house. My father, who had a fine sense of pitch, complained bitterly when she continued to sing a certain note just a little off key. However I loved it, since I lacked the ability to be as discerning.

Aunt Ilse who was also asthmatic was sent to Italy when she was twelve because she could not endure the damp cold winters of Northern Germany. She was sent all alone to a *pensione* in Italy then and never forgave my grandmother for this exile.

However my Aunt Ilse's frailty remained a constant concern even in her adult life. She had pneumonia and my grandmother came to help with her care. Then she became pregnant and the baby died during a difficult home delivery. Her next two children were born in a hospital, not a common practice then.

She and I had a common bond, our love of exploring new ideas. She studied Chinese poetry, and even in her seventies in America she took a furniture making course and did very well in it. She had studied painting in Italy. I remember postcards from those days that she sent me from San Remo, and she painted ardently all her life. She visited museums and participated in debates about the art trends of the time. She was also an expert bridge player to the end of her life, and playing bridge is a passion of mine as well.

In Hamburg, there was another painter in the family, my mother's cousin Edith Marcus. Her mother Helene was my grandmother's sister. We would take a boat to visit them where they lived in Altona, an excursion up the Elbe River.

Edith Marcus was a painter of stature and had won awards. Impressionism and subsequent art trends came through in her paintings. My father who was very interested in art though not schooled in it, loved her paintings and commissioned a large portrait of my mother in the early days of their marriage. In addition he bought other paintings of hers.

One of these was a scene of the Fish Market in Hamburg (which I remember first-hand as an evil-smelling, wet, slimy place). The painting my father bought romanticized the Fish Market, but I remember it differently, with cold water running down between the stalls, and glistening fresh fish with staring dead eyes!

I also remember visiting the famous Hamburg Zoo. I have never liked zoos but this was an unacceptable position within my family, especially to my father who ardently loved them, and who loved anything having to do with animals.

But I did not like seeing the animals caged up, and that spoiled whatever pleasure I might have had from visiting this famous zoo. I would look at the lions trapped in their pens and the tigers pacing up and down, the polar bears in the scummy green water that emitted a smell more hideous than the fish market, and beg to go home.

Even the patient elephants lifting their open pink warm trunks at me for their reward of peanuts failed to make me happy at the zoo. All I could think of was how miserable the animals must be, trapped in their too-small cages and unnatural enclosures. To this day I dislike zoos.

But there were also circuses in Hamburg and a flea circus was a special children's treat along with puppet theaters. I loved watching the acrobats, especially on horseback, but my favorites were the puppets. Aside from my dislike of seeing animals caged up, I was easily entertained.

CHAPTER SEVEN

MY PARENTS

My mother was the youngest in her family. Fatherless before she was ten, she grew up surrounded by three brothers and an exceedingly powerful, competent, intelligent mother. She attended finishing school and learned to run a large household with the servants that were available at the time.

Her personal passion was sports. She particularly loved tennis and spent hours practicing her backhand and forehand against a backboard. She was a fiercely competitive player. Although her physique was short and broad with wide hips, she ran mercilessly after shots that appeared hopeless to me. She was tireless when it came to athletics. She also rarely showed her soft side to me.

I was not close to my mother when I was a child. With my mother's main interest being sports, motherhood must have been a distant second, if that. In addition I (she made clear to me) had none of the attributes or abilities she would have valued in a daughter.

Some of my earliest memories involve failure of some sort on my part. One of these is of being allowed to carry a potty filled by my little baby sister

Susi who was being trained in its purpose. Since we were a year and three months apart I must have been between three and four years old.

I fell and the porcelain potty broke, spilling its contents onto the parquet floor. And I severely cut the middle finger of my right hand. (I still bear the scar. For many years it helped me tell my right from my left hand.) My feeling that I was clumsy began quite early.

Originally according to family lore, I was left-handed. This was considered undesirable and inconvenient back then, and so every time I picked anything up it was shifted to the desired right hand until I began to use my right hand myself. Discouragement of left-handedness in children was common then. I would especially pay a price for this in the first grade when I was first learning to write.

I also remember the Christmas of 1929 or 1930, which as assimilated Jews my family had no problem celebrating; although this Christmas memory is not a pleasant one. I even believed in Santa Claus back then.

One December evening the door bell rand and I was urged to open it, accompanied by our maid Lisbet, my parents, and Uncle Erwin. There, filling up the doorway, was Santa Claus clad in his red suit and red hat with white trim, just as I had seen him in picture books!

But although Santa looked jolly he carried a switch made of bare twigs tied together. From the branches dangled some candies. Santa informed me that the switch was for me, because I had been a bad girl!

I was mortified and stood in silence. Someone told me to say thank you, but I just cried. This may have seemed like innocent fun to the adults but even now I consider it a sad, twisted incident of my German girlhood. Our maid Lisbet, who I never liked, may have been the culprit who planned Santa's visit and the mixed messages it brought, although I cannot say for sure.

❧

To be clear I was no angel as a child, but this was due more to my curiosity, which was enormous, than any desire to make trouble. If anything, I craved adult approval because I received little of it.

Because I was curious about everything I couldn't understand (and children, even bright ones, do not understand a lot), when not supervised I was frequently involved in unapproved activities. Some were artistic in nature, or so I thought.

Once I cut out the embroidered flowers on my mother's dance frock because they were beautiful and I wanted to keep them. I still remember the white dress with lovely embroidered flowers circling the floor length skirt.

My interest in my dolls was more mechanical than artistic. These dolls generally ended up in a drawer called the hospital drawer because when they were laid down their eyelids closed automatically, and I was fascinated with that and tried to see how this worked by forcing their eyes open and closed. As a result every one of my dolls' eyes eventually dropped into her body, and soon a row of sightless dolls would lie there in the drawer, silently accusing me! My mother would be furious and not listen to my explanations.

My father was in his own way as preoccupied as my mother but he had a gentler, more patient way with me. Perhaps he understood my curiosity better, since he had a lot of that himself.

In the mornings I loved to watch my father shave. He was a tall man, about six foot two or three, and he had a very low bass voice. He was meticulous in his habits and compulsive about cleanliness.

My father finally married my mother when he was 36, and after much hesitation. He was a careful man in every respect and little given to impulse. In his youth he and his friends loved the outdoors in summer for fishing and hiking and in the winter for skiing.

He told me once with great delight - his fascination still evident - about one of his youthful friends who had been able to catch fish with his bare hands, to the admiration of all the boys. I believe that my father's soul remained in the mountains all his life and even throughout all our travels. He was attached to nature in almost a mystical way.

He knew the plants, their names, and their unique qualities. He was familiar with wild animals and felt a bond with them. He knew the mountain trails and was a tireless walker. Much of his feeling for nature was spiritual; being within nature always restored him in difficult times.

As soon as I could walk, my father began taking me into the mountains for hikes that were frequently too arduous for my short legs. While he talked with the other men on the hiking trails, I found nettles that irritated my skin and berries and mushrooms that soiled my clothes. And unable to yet share his enthusiasm for the glories of the mountains I soon grew tired and cranky and asked to be carried. Still he persisted at introducing me to nature and I eventually came to share his love for it.

When my father shaved we played a game together. His shaving knife was in a rectangular case, neatly folded. He would say:"Open Sesame!" Lo and behold, the metal box opened and the shaving knife unfolded itself. I never tired of this little game. I always tried to find out how it was done. One day when I was close to four I found the tiny bump that needed pressing to release the mechanism and I too could make it work! For better or worse, as with the dolls I broke, I was always fascinated with how things worked.

My maternal grandmother, Adele, was a regular visitor in the early days of my childhood. She had tremendous influence on my mother who revered her, and on my father who respected her. She was there when babies were born, when serious illnesses occurred, and when advice was needed.

Back then there were no 'How To' books on baby care. So a continuous exchange of letters took place between my mother and my grandmother regarding the serious business of civilizing a wild child like myself.

The goal, I realized early on, was nothing short of perfection. The price was high. When it was discovered that I was somewhat knock-kneed I was dispatched to an orthopedist whose office was located in the nearest large city from Pforzheim, Baden Baden. This doctor placed my left (or was it my right?) leg in a metal cast, up to the hip. It hurt like hell. I remember standing in my crib with the metal cast. It was impossible to get comfortable.

Another unacceptable habit of mine was that I sucked the middle finger of my right hand. According to conventional wisdom then, this was a serious problem that could cause a disfiguring change in the bite; a deformed middle finger, and a possible problem for the lips. So every night both my hands were bound with large white man's handkerchiefs, leaving me, with my constant winter colds, to sniffle hopelessly.

But the most torturous remedies of the day were the sweat baths my sister and I endured whenever we were ill with a fever. For these, we were wrapped in ice cold sheets and then covered with wool blankets and surrounded by hot water bottles to sweat it all out. No aspirin, no antibiotics, only a Spartan sweat bath regimen. Fortunately we were rarely ill.

Our food intake was also rigidly supervised. It consisted of hot cereals and bread and butter in the mornings. Then there would be a hot meal at noon when my father came home from the factory. That consisted of soup, meat (generally stewed or boiled, rarely roasted) vegetables (usually root vegetables because of the storage facilities during the long winter), potatoes in various forms (usually boiled), bread and butter, and pudding of some sort for desert. Other than that there were no sweets, cookies, cakes or other temptations.

On Sundays however we were permitted to share the grownups' bounty as long as we were polite and kissed all the aunts and uncles, thanked them sweetly for any gifts, and curtsied on entering and leaving their presence.

Back then there were absolutely no weight problems among either the children or the adults, since everyone's diet consisted of whole, natural foods and very few sweets or processed foods. We were allowed apples, which were stored in the cellar for an occasional snack between meals. In the evening for our supper we ate cottage cheese, with bread and butter and berries or stewed fruit. Junk food, fast food and the like didn't exist back then.

Our bread was never white, except at parties. Otherwise it was whole wheat, rye, or pumpernickel. In just about every way my childhood diet was healthier and consisted of more whole foods than what children eat nowadays.

CHAPTER EIGHT

SUSI

Three months before my second birthday my baby sister arrived. With her came a baby nurse I still recall. She wore a voluminous navy blue outfit and a complicated headdress of navy and a white starched frame around her face. She had a soft gentle voice for the baby and for me. She allowed me to help with the baby. I had never met anyone quite like her. She sang, read stories, and recited nursery rhymes. We took the baby out in the buggy and I wheeled my doll in her buggy alongside. My baby sister became the most exciting event I could remember. She was admired for her long lashed dark eyes and her beautiful dark curly hair.

After some months the baby nurse left, and my sister gradually expanded her territory from the crib and baby buggy into the realm of my toys and pastimes. Suddenly she was no longer docile and adorable. A new young woman was hired to look after the two of us. Quite authoritarian and inflexible, she began to rule us with great emphasis on order, cleanliness, and discipline.

My parents were delighted with her greater control over us. "Lisbet," they would tell my aunts and uncles," . . . has done wonders with the children. She has made little ladies out of little savages." But Lisbet had no warmth and I disliked her.

One day my sister, a little past age two, took a walk in the garden. Through a gate left open by a delivery man she walked out of the garden and kept going. It was late fall and darkness arrived early. Eventually her absence was discovered. Terror reigned because the Lindbergh case had alerted parents everywhere to the danger always within reach.

In my sister's case she was fortunate. A policeman saw her walking happily by herself and took her down to the station. When my frantic parents came to pick her up, she was enjoying herself, entertained and fed by the men, and she wailed loudly when she had to leave. After that venture of hers, we were no longer allowed to play alone and unwatched. Everywhere we went we were monitored by Lisbet or another adult.

Just before my fourth birthday a new baby was born to Aunt Ilse and Uncle Erwin. His name was Walter. Since we lived in the same house all I needed to do was to walk upstairs to visit. He too had a baby nurse I liked and I found him fascinating. His hair was light blond and softly curly. My parents and all the aunts and uncles celebrated the first boy in the family. I was aware almost since I could remember how disappointed they all felt that I was a girl; especially my mother found that difficult to accept for a very long time.

Now that I was four I could visit with my aunt and see baby Walter who lived upstairs from us. And I could go up still another flight and visit my grandmother Helene who had her apartment at the very top of the house. My grandmother would greet me with embarrassment when I rang the door bell because she did not have her false teeth in place. These sat in a glass at her bedside table. I was fascinated by their appearance when they sat with the pink gums in the water and the white even teeth looking ready to bite. I loved watching them disappear into my grandmother's mouth.

I learned to knit and crochet in my grandmother's apartment. Since her eyesight was failing due to her cataracts, I threaded her needles when she mended. One of my favorite jobs was to use her buttonhooks on the buttons of her winter boots. She wore a corset with bone stays and when she dressed she held on to the bedpost while I pulled on the pink string.

She would have me pull tighter and tighter until her white breasts lay upon the stiff top like soft dough mounds. I knew very well that this was disapproved of by my mother as unhealthy vanity but it was lovely to watch my grandmother get dressed in her silk dress, generally black with a pale lilac chiffon scarf around her throat and her wealth of while hair fluffed and dressed in a mound resembling meringue atop her head.

Grandmother Helene carried herself like a queen, everyone said. She was almost painfully proud of her sons' success in the world; and because of that, her pain when we all had to leave Germany must have been enormous. As it was, she was among the last in our family to accept that we had to go.

At times I would be playing in a distant part of the garden. I would hear my grandmother calling me, *"Reni, Reni!"* It was my nickname. Everyone called me *Reni* or *Renimausie* or sometimes just *Mausie*. I can hear my voice in that long ago time drifting back to my grandmother over the trees and bushes, "I'm in America, *Grossma*!" That was as far away as I could imagine.

Little did I know in those happy, fleeting childhood days that I would actually be in America all too soon and not by choice. It would have made my grandmother cry, I'm sure, to even think of that.

CHAPTER NINE

STARTING SCHOOL IN PFORZEIM

O ne day my mother announced to me I was now a big girl and it was time for me to go to school! A picture taken of me on my first day of school shows me with a brand new plaid school dress, a backpack for the schoolbooks and a large cone of colored paper filled with candy and other treats, a Pforzheim custom for a brand new scholar on the early path to knowledge. The cone filled with candy, as it turned out, was the only sweet thing about my new school experience, which was otherwise miserable.

Excited, I walked the long way to the schoolhouse that first day without realizing I had started on a lifelong path that would take me far away from Pforzheim. And while I later came to love learning, my first forays into education were neither easy nor enjoyable. In fact, I soon came to hate school.

I had not attended kindergarten because my family had kept me at home as company for my sister and cousin Walter. Therefore I lacked any of the skills my classmates had learned in kindergarten. For example I had never held a pen, cut out paper, folded paper or mastered any of the other basic tasks now required. My natural left-handedness also probably interfered as I tried quickly to catch up.

Till now I had been sheltered in the sometimes harsh but at least predictable environment of home and family. Once I began school there was more severity than predictability, and worse, none of the approval I still craved.

Worse, I did not know any of my new schoolmates. One subject I had to master right away was German script. Each letter had to be carefully formed with a pen dipped in an inkwell. The letters were ornate with pronounced down strokes and carefully formed loops. Mine were blotches that could not be erased. I tried to erase them with an ink eraser and wound up with holes in the paper.

We made pen wipers in class to clean the tips of the pens, as they accumulated gritty material that stopped the smooth flow of the ink. Alas, even so my six year old hand would not steady on the page; my ink failed to flow in an even stream, and large ink blots marred my painful efforts. These then resisted my desperate efforts at erasure, which frequently led to even more disaster.

Soon the teacher called my mother to school to complain about my lack of ability and my disgraceful penmanship. I was required to stay after school and continue practicing my letters. Daily I felt ashamed and clumsy compared to my schoolmates.

Our teacher also inspected the class for cleanliness each morning. We had to show our hands, both sides. In that class of mostly blonde, blue eyed, fair skinned children my mother's Sephardic heritage loomed large.

I felt painfully out of place. My hair was dark brown, my eyes even darker brown, and my complexion olive. The teacher never found my hands clean enough, no matter how strenuous my efforts. And I longed, impossibly, for fair skin, blue eyes, and blonde braids.

At ten each morning we had a class called simply religion. The religion studied was not mine. I sat on the school steps with another outsider, a Christian Scientist. We never spoke. Both of us probably felt too excluded to attempt any social interaction. Disconsolately alone at opposite ends of the steps we waited quietly- outcasts in a Lutheran world.

Reading and arithmetic proved more accessible subjects. Still I felt like an unwelcome stranger in the school atmosphere and soon came to detest school wholeheartedly, despite my natural curiosity and thirst to learn.

My parents took no notice. Their world was falling apart in a way I was unaware of and could not possibly have understood. But my own world felt pretty dismal.

❀

Just about then another new baby arrived -- a delightful addition to our household. My cousin Ann was a beautiful little sister to my cousin Walter. My sister Susi and I took turns checking up on the baby. We vied to help with her care. I was happy at home in the presence of this precious new baby even while increasingly miserable at school.

Given my continuing school difficulties combined with my excitement over the new baby, it took some time for me to realize that extreme changes, not for the better, were impacting the grown-ups around me.

Before now my orderly home life had given me a certain respite from the unpleasantness of school. Now though, as I sensed that the worsening mood in our household might be here to stay, home no longer offered the comfort I so badly needed.

CHAPTER TEN

OUR FAMILY'S LUCK RUNS OUT

I t wasn't one thing or another that suddenly changed at our house; it was many little things that slowly but steadily made the whole atmosphere tense and unpleasant.

My increasingly preoccupied parents started treating the servants in a distant, distracted manner. I was spanked when I refused to eat an offered soup. My mother and father stopped their usual lighthearted banter with my aunt and uncle and with my grandmother. Sunday gatherings changed from happy festive ones to tense, anxious sessions where tempers were short. For reasons no one would tell me, none of the adults were any longer enjoying life.

My first memories of all these changes were connected with the radio. Everyone began gathering around it with what seemed like religious devotion. The rasping metallic voices that emanated from that rectangular black box became all-important to the adults, much more so than the voices of us children who wanted to be heard too but were now drowned out. We were interfering with important things the adults needed to hear.

I was taken to visit relatives I had not seen much before. One day we visited Aunt Auguste. She lived in an apartment with her two deaf mute twin brothers, for whom she kept house. The brothers worked in the jewelry industry, like many Pforzheim residents. My mother told me that Aunt Auguste lived mostly on coffee and eggs from her chickens. She was tiny and slim and offered me cookies and candy. She resembled my grandmother Helene, who was her cousin.

For Aunt Auguste there were new problems regarding the continued employment of her brothers. When the brothers entered the house I remember being a little afraid because their voices sounded quite unlike any I had ever heard before. They had little inflection or modulation and their spoken words had a flat mechanical-sounding cadence.

About now also, my mother began to seem more distant and preoccupied than ever. Susi and I spent even more time with Lisbet, who was increasingly strict and demanding. I began to feel even more alone with my thoughts, feelings and unanswered questions.

About now I first grew keenly interested in the books my Uncle Werner sent me, in order to escape the heavy atmosphere of home. I began to read avidly, which grew into a lifelong habit.

Susi, Walter and I also spent more time than ever playing by ourselves in the garden since there wasn't anything else to do. No one took us anywhere, brought us anything or noticed us much anymore. So we played day after day in the sand box and spent a lot of time jumping on the warm compost heap in back of the property. The adults had their world and we had ours.

One day Walter was stung on the tongue by a bee and his cries took a long while to rouse anyone. Formerly someone would have come running at once, but now we children were on our own. Even Susi's and my expensive, well-appointed baby buggies were left out in the rain and the dolls tucked inside them drenched and ruined. No one bothered bringing such items in from the weather anymore; everyone had more important things to do.

My maternal grandmother Adele came for a visit and for the first time ever she had no inclination to play with me. Instead she spent her days with us talking, talking, talking to the adults and became angry when I sought her attention.

Eventually I grew sulky from all the neglect. I began fighting with my sister, and that further upset the adults. Though I was still too young to understand the cause-and-effect of it all, I did come to understand that as Jews we were no longer welcome in Germany.

Even so I still had to go to school. At the end of the school year I passed, through sheer persistence and hard work, all of my subjects: German script, reading, arithmetic, German grammar, and singing. Singing unfortunately was not a strong ability of mine, much to my chagrin because I loved it. My father had a pleasant base voice and on our outings he would sing traditional German songs to me. To his great disappointment though, I could not carry a tune.

❋

That spring my father and uncle also received a telegram from their brother Rudolf who had left Germany as a very young man, married and settled in Chile. His wife Regina and their six children came to visit. I remember the oldest, named Helene after my grandmother and the youngest, whose name was Jorge.

In order to greet them all, the house was decorated with evergreen garlands and bore an inscription of welcome. But communication was difficult since the wife spoke only a little German and we could not speak Spanish.

Still, my grandmother and Aunt Tala were ecstatic to see them all. My father and uncle soon learned however that their long-absent brother was in serious financial trouble, and was even borrowing money from their own friends and business clients. The visit terminated abruptly after that and no further news of Rudolf or his family ever came.

Such brief appearances and disappearances were typical then. Everything and everybody was unsettled - inside and outside our house. And we were learning that what the adults said was often less important than what they did not.

CHAPTER ELEVEN

LEAVING PFORZHEIM

Before long a terrible depression settled like a gray woolen blanket over the adults of our household. The jewelry business my father and uncle had built with such effort was becoming impossible to sustain.

It happened in daily increments. First my father's and uncle's employees began growing openly hostile to a Jewish owner. Suppliers then became a problem. Without loyal employees and steady suppliers a business fails. A business is also a community affair and none can survive without community support. Gradually my father's and uncle's moods grew as cloudy as a gathering storm.

As difficult as all this was for us children, it must have been nearly unbearable for the adults. Our own lives were just beginning; but for them, this *was* life—the best, and now the worst, that life had to offer. Life in this place had blessed them once but now it had viciously turned on them.

And not taking it personally was not an option because often it *was* personal. My father and uncle had it worst since theirs were such public lives. My father's work, his friendships, his reputation and his good name (a Jewish name to be sure; but that had not hurt him before now) were all he had. Now he was being diminished day by day.

His boyhood friends, the companions of his youth, who had hiked and fished, skied and skated, rode horses with him and gone dancing with him, stopped even greeting him in the streets. Instead they crossed the street to avoid him.

He began coming home every day in a black mood that filled even our huge household like suffocating smoke. After all, he had once ditched school with these same people who now wouldn't even say hello as he walked home from an honest day's work. He had once shared meals and drinks with these same people who now avoided him on the street. As young adults some of them had risked their lives together in the First World War. After that my father had worked with some of them.

My father could never accept the change, only observe it. Sometimes he confronted his former friends. "Max, the times have changed!" they would say, thereby excusing themselves.

But one thing became increasingly clear to my father. The times weren't going to change back in his favor.

So my father began to search for a place to resettle. He decided on Holland.

CHAPTER TWELVE

OUR DUTCH SUMMER

In the summer of 1932 my mother and father found a small apartment in the seaside town of Zaandvort, Holland which they rented. It was furnished and located at street level. Our maid Lisbet brought my sister and me to join them.

The summer temperature was cool and the dunes were damp, and Holland was an expensive place to live because of the exchange rates.

After we'd settled in my grandmother Adele came to visit. She wore the usual black silk dress and high boots that were closed with small round buttons for which she used a metal button hook.

When we visited the beach that summer Grandmother Adele liked to sit in a large rented beach chair that provided shade.

One day during one of the innumerable adult discussions of the political and social problems that had brought us here; I wandered away into the salty shallow water that the outgoing tide had left. I played in the water and behold-I discovered that it bore me. I floated! I was so enchanted with this discovery I forgot about the outgoing tide and then had to paddle furiously to return to the shore.

We also bicycled in Holland. One day my father put me on the handlebars of his bicycle and my right foot became caught in the spokes. He pedaled harder, not knowing this, and I was too stunned by the increasing pain of my twisted ankle to even cry out at first. After that ill-fated ride we found a Dutch doctor who repaired the damage to my ankle, but a large scar remained.

We found the Dutch language similar to the Plattdeutsch spoken in parts of Hamburg. Soon my sister and I began to play with the Dutch children.

Several lived in an apartment above us. Like children in any country we would all meet in the street or down the block. Susi and I found the rope skipping games and the counting games full of camaraderie. Sometimes it almost seemed like home in Pforzheim, only better. Dutch people of all ages were friendly, accepting folks.

But some obviously had their problems too, like in Germany or anywhere else. One evening during our usual playtime in the streets we heard loud adult shouting. A window above where we were playing flew open and within minutes, piece after piece of heavy furniture came crashing down into the street!

From what we could tell a marital battle was in full force above us. The next day, in the mysterious way adults had of coming and going (and that Susi and I were now used to) we found the upstairs apartment with last night's noisy adults deserted, and some of our favorite little friends gone.

My father had business dealings in Holland and explored the possibility of permanent refuge there for us. However the high exchange rate and the cool windy weather and dampness were not to his liking. So ultimately he decided against Holland as our new home. Still, I have fond, if fleeting, memories of our summer there.

CHAPTER THIRTEEN

TO HAMBURG

We moved instead back to Germany, this time to Hamburg, my mother's home town, on a temporary basis. My father was rarely with us anymore by now and my mother, sister and I lived in my grandmother's house. Susi and I were enrolled in a new school, this time one for Jewish children.

The weather on the North Sea was cold and rainy and the wind carried wet leaves along the sodden streets. School here was quite different from my previous one, but in a whole new way even more unpleasant than Pforzheim.

At this school there was no Lutheran religion class for me to be awkwardly excluded from; instead (even more oddly) there were Hebrew prayers throughout the day.

Like many well-assimilated German Jewish families, mine was not a religious one. Up to now my experience with praying had been limited to a simple *Sh'ma*. So I actually knew nothing of the Hebrew alphabet or of the strange Hebrew songs my new Hamburg schoolmates from religious families sang effortlessly.

Again I was intimidated, but for whole new reasons. In this new environment I found myself struggling to adjust and survive. I missed my toys. I missed our house and garden and most of all I missed my cousins, Walter and Annie, and their parents and my other grandmother, and gentle, loving Aunt Tala.

As difficult as I found the adjustment to Hamburg, I believe it was even harder for Susi. My younger sister had turned into a shy child and like all timid children she especially hated change. And increasingly that was all we knew.

Susi soon developed serious eating problems because the food here in Hamburg was so different from what we were used to in Pforzheim.

She also contrived strategies of pocketing her chewed up portion or stuffing unwanted food into the potted palms at my grandmother's house. And then she was teased by my uncles because of her shyness.

I grew protective of her. She was so helpless and looking out for her distracted me from my own troubles. At night when I could not sleep and counted the peals of the church bells and the number of street cars that passed, I would try my new Jewish prayers to see if those would help. They never did.

Hamburg was also a much more stylish, sophisticated place than Pforzheim. So Susi and I acquired new clothes that were more attractive than any we'd owned before.

I remember a camel's hair coat with a matching hat and spats to keep our feet warm and dry. Plaid dresses with white collars were the usual dress for school. These were worn with long brown stockings held up by garters attached to our undergarments. Brown shoes (usually covered by galoshes because of the frequent rain) completed the look.

We also had umbrellas that we carried everywhere to ward off the rain.

Shopping in Hamburg was much different than in Pforzheim. Here the stores were large and filled with wonderful toys. Moving window displays of toy trains and Christmas scenes shone from the decorated, colorfully lit streets.

Days grew short as fall turned into winter, and I remember that the brightly lit houses of Hamburg with their tall green Christmas trees, nativity scenes and advent calendars were especially beautiful. Displays of dried fruits and candies in the Hamburg stores fascinated me, especially the marzipan fruits and flowers, animals, and little objects I recognized from the farms back in Pforzheim, including baskets and milking stools.

Christmas packages people carried in the streets were wrapped in colorful paper with huge bows. My uncles would tease me about being provincial, with a broad Bavarian accent. So I tried to be more stylish and absorb the ways of Hamburg.

My greatest delight in this new city was the entertainment. This included puppet theaters; operettas, the flea circus, ballets for children and much more. I also loved to go to the cold and smelly but picturesque Fish Market, where women hawked their wares with great gusto in the broad *Plaatdeutsch* language.

The smell of the Fish Market was powerful, and you had to step gingerly to avoid the streaming rivers of melting ice strongly laced with fishy odors. The variety of seafood was also incredible. I had never seen anything resembling the colors, shapes, and sizes of marine life—huge fish of all kinds and colors, including ugly black wormlike eels with snarling faces and dangerous looking fangs. And there were clams, mussels, oysters, shrimp, crabs, squid and octopus.

In Hamburg we also met some new cousins. Susi and I were shy because of our less sophisticated ways and thoroughly impressed with the daring and confidence of the big city kids.

Once there was a family holiday dinner at my grandmother's house. We all sat down at an enormous dining table and delicacies unknown to me were served: smoked eel and oysters, caviar, tiny crackers with pate, a beautiful goose with apple stuffing, delicate rolls, condiments, cakes and cookies.

Although I had the run of the house while I lived there the kitchen was forbidden territory and neither I nor any of my cousins ever saw the inside of it. The house was very large, suitable for a family with five active children - my sister, me, and three of our cousins. Built of grey stone, it had a staircase going up in the center like our old house in Pforzheim.

My favorite room was upstairs. Called the conservatory, it was a library with a large skylight. The room had a wonderful grand piano on which my Uncle Werner sometimes played Chopin.

Before anti-Semitism grew intense my grandmother had a Christmas tree decorated with little white candles, edible ornaments for the children, and little presents beneath the tree for the servants. My mother's family was not religious until the persecution of the Jews.

But after Hitler came to power, being singled out as Jewish caused my uncles and aunts to study Hebrew and Jewish history in order to try to understand the roots of the hatred. I'm not sure if that really helped them understand it better. How do you understand the irrational? But like a lot of adults back then they were doing their best to make sense of what was essentially incomprehensible.

During our sojourn in Hamburg my father sought to liquidate whatever he could from his business and prepare for our exile. He packed and shipped all of the company records, the wonderful drawings of the various jewelry pieces designed by the firm; the diamond scales, the little scoops for sorting and all other equipment needed for his business. All this must have broken his heart but he was very cold-blooded about it. There was no other choice.

My father also ordered the packing and shipping of much of the furniture in our house in Pforzheim to a storage facility in Switzerland. This part of our preparations to leave Germany caused him great anguish. Many of the little ornaments, the pictures, trinkets, and mementos he had bought with my mother, the tiny personal irreplaceable things that made up their life together were stolen during this process.

I doubt that the thieves, whoever they were, cared or even thought for a second how losing such precious items would hurt my parents. I doubt they thought of us as people anything like themselves. This was what Germany had become.

CHAPTER FOURTEEN

LEAVING GERMANY

A nd then, after our long wrenching preparations to leave, came our final train ride out of Germany. With all my father had sold from his business we were now among the lucky few German Jewish families able to buy our way abroad before it became too late. That said; good luck never felt so bad.

We were headed for Italy this time, to a whole new country and way of life. The sad, painful parts of our family odyssey were far from over, though, and the train ride out of Germany was no picnic either.

My mother, my father, my sister Sue and I sat together in a train compartment, our suitcases stowed around us. We felt tense and anxious beyond description. Even with all our papers in order, we had no idea what would happen tomorrow or the day after or even in the next few minutes.

My parents, and my father especially, were well organized clear thinkers and probably, out of necessity, exquisitely good planners.

But there is no way to plan the leaving behind of every person, place and object you have ever known.

So— you choose the day you will leave; you leave, and you hope for the best.

You know you have no choice.

Inside your head you are *glad* you can leave since so many others cannot; and you know they may die in some horrible way you cannot bear to think about.

Still your heart is breaking because you do not want to leave and if it was up to you, you would not.

But it is not up to you.

●

On the train out of Germany my parents do not talk to each other or to us. We are quiet. We feel beaten, intimidated. Have we not lost all?

At the border leaving Germany a German soldier enters our cabin and orders my father to go to the station to be searched. Then they come for my mother. She, too, leaves to be searched.

Now Sue and I are all alone on the train.

Sue and I sit in speechless terror until finally my father returns.

But my mother is still gone.

After what seems a week my mother is back. Her cheeks are deep red.

She cannot bear to look at any of us.

My father gently knifes open the palpable silence. "What happened?" he asks.

"They took me into a room and made me strip and searched every orifice, including vaginal and anal."

My father cringes. He would be angry if we weren't here, away from home. Anger is an emotion we can't spend here.

My mother is still shaking visibly.

My sister and I are terrified.

We have been told earlier by Papa to hold onto a particular small black suitcase. It is cheap shiny black with a light beige waterproof lining of the kind you put wet bathing suits into after a day at the beach. Ah, the beach!

There are diamonds in the lining of the cheap black suitcase we are later told when we are all safe in Italy.

The secret, which we children do not know, is not discovered.

We proceed to Italy.

We have smuggled our anger, our sadness, and our diamonds out.

I was born into a multi-generational household. Left: My cousin Ann as a baby on the balcony of our house in Pforzheim, Germany, circa 1932. Right: my paternal grandmother Helene, still beautiful in her 80s. She lived upstairs from our family.

My mother is on the far left and her sister my aunt Ilse is on the far right on an outing with friends, circa 1916.

In Germany circa 1928: Left to right: Uncle Sepp (Joseph Rosenfeld, my father's sister Tala's husband), Aunt Tala (Natalia Rosenfeld); Uncle Erwin (standing); Grandmother Helene (seated), Aunt Ilse, me, Grandmother Adele (my mother's mother), my baby sister Susi, my mother Eleanor and my father Max. My earliest memories are of a household that included not just my parents and sister but Grandmother Helene, Aunt Ilse, Uncle Erwin, and my cousins Walter and Ann.

Grandmother Helene (center) loved to entertain relatives and friends on Kaffe Klatch Sundays in Pforz-heim. She was proud of my father and uncle's success. Uncle Sepp is on the far left, and my dad Max is next to him. Next to my dad is an unknown guest. My uncle Erwin is on my grandmother's left, and my mother is on her right. To my mother's right is another unknown guest.

My father and my uncle Erwin both loved the outdoors. Here they are with their riding club in Germany before their friends began to shun them for being Jewish. Uncle Erwin is third from the left and my father fourth from the left.

Looking ahead seriously. Left: My sister Susi age 2. Right: Me at 3 1/2.

My father was always a good dresser. Here he is in Germany in 1927 or 1928.

This is me in Pforzheim at five years old pouring tea.

My first cousins Ann and Walter with their nanny in 1934

Still smiling: Six first cousins gathered around a scooter in the early 1930s. Left to right: Walter, me, Alfred, Anne, Susi and Gisela. Only Walter looks wary here, but before long the rest of us wouldn't smile much either. Alfred and Gisela are the children of my mother's brother Gerhardt.

Taken in Alleghe, Italy in the mid-1930s after we had fled Germany, this picture captures the essence of my maternal grandmother Adele's quiet strength.

This was taken in Florence, Italy in 1937 before my aunt Ilse and uncle Erwin left Italy with my cousins for America. We followed next. Left to right are Aunt Ilse, Uncle Erwin, Grandmother Adele, me, Susi, my mother, my father, Ann and Walter.

As a UC Berkeley student I reluctantly attended a dance where I met a handsome young naval officer named Sam Rosenthal who became my husband! I'm glad I went!

Sam and I were married April 1, 1945.

Me in my wedding gown

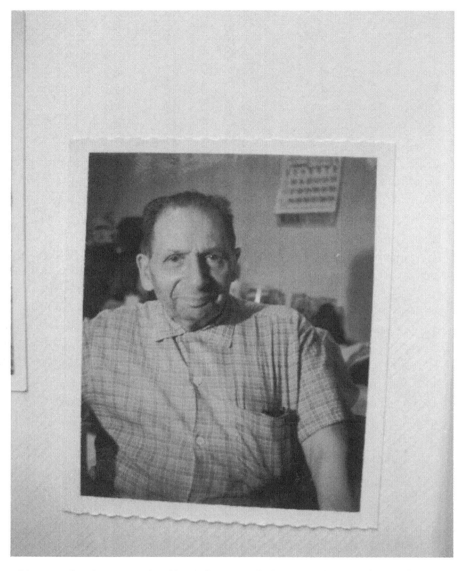

My maternal uncle, Ernst, in whose New York apartment building I stayed when my husband Sam was stationed overseas in World War II.

Uncle Ernst (left) outside the United Nations Building in 1938 with family friends.

My parents adjusted with difficulty to life in America, though they put a brave and dignified face on things, as they do here. Not till I was much older did I realize the extent of the sacrifices they made as middle aged immigrants for their children's sake. This was taken in 1941 or 1942.

Barbara was born in 1950 and Michael in 1947. Their Southern California childhoods were very different from mine.

Left: My parents in their later years. Right: Me with my father Max and son Michael in Palm Springs on vacation in 1949.

This is Sam and me today. My smile says it all.

CHAPTER FIFTEEN

ARRIVING IN ITALY

We arrived in Florence, or as we soon learned to call it, *Firenze*, in late summer. My father was still not entirely sure this was goodbye forever to his beloved mountains; his skiing, his friends from youth. He still hoped not.

We hoped the same. Or maybe it was just that none of us could bear the thought that this was it - goodbye to Germany forever.

In Italy foreigners could not work, so in order for us to live my father sold the diamonds from the black suitcase he had saved from the goods he used in his factory. Jews were not allowed to take anything valuable out of Germany.

Our first home in Florence was a *pensione*. It was a large home that had been remodeled into a rooming house by an enterprising German Jewish couple. It housed mostly Jewish refugees.

Meals were served in a large dining room. Maids took care of the beds, towels, etc. and washed for a small number of extra *lire*. The house was set in a very large, exceptionally beautiful garden. I remember the big lovely lawn, the rose arbor which consisted of a table surrounded by benches in a round, trellised structure covered by white baby roses in full bloom of profuse enchanting fragrance.

I loved to read there in the shade. On one side was a hedge trimmed about waist high. Summer nights it filled with fireflies flickering in a magical display. There was a vegetable garden-out of bounds for us but interesting because it was full of squash, tomatoes, cucumbers, lettuce, rosemary, and basil. There were lemon and orange trees, truly exotic to a little girl from the cold north of Germany.

The other refugees were wonderful to us. The women played with us and told us stories. The men teased us and did magic tricks.

Next door to our *pensione* was a large estate that belonged to an Italian count, Signor Giachetti. His wife and daughters were visiting in England for the summer. The count's wife was English. They returned to their estate at the end of the summer and our family got to know them then.

The count himself had fought in the Italian army in Eritrea and had a lame leg as a result. So he walked leaning heavily on a walking stick. He formed a strong attachment to us, especially my mother. He was also kind to my sister and me.

He had a beautiful large library in his home and allowed me to read whatever I wanted. I began with the *Dr. Doolittle* books, in Italian, which I was just beginning to learn. We sat in the garden and talked, he teaching me Italian, I teaching him German. When my father was away on business trips to Holland and Switzerland in an effort to sell the merchandize he had saved, Signor Giachetti would make my mother's exile from her friends and family less painful. They spoke in English since my mother had not yet acquired much Italian.

My aunt Ilse and my uncle Erwin and their children had also come to Italy by then and found an apartment some distance away and uphill from us. My aunt was suffering from severe asthma during that time and my uncle was traveling like my father. Although we saw my cousins it was no longer daily. So my sister and I became very close. We invented long complicated fantasy games. She was the mother, fashionable and worldly, and I was the baby. We made up codes to signal dislike of some of the other tenants at the *pensione*, especially the men who like to pinch us or hold us too long on their laps.

That same summer my grandmother Adele came to visit, and she also stayed at the *pensione*. The news she brought was discouraging but she still insisted she would never leave her home. Then my uncle Werner came to visit.

He flew over the Alps in an airplane and I can still recall the wonder I felt when he described soaring high in the air over the peaks. It was the first time I heard of someone flying in a plane.

In the fall my parents took an apartment on *Via Senese 16A*. We lived upstairs from a wonderful Italian family with a teenage son. We had a balcony in the back of the apartment and a smaller balcony in the front that faced the street. The floors were made of marble and the apartment was heated with a wood burning stove in the central hall. We cooked with charcoal.

The apartment consisted of a bedroom for my parents, a shared bedroom for Susi and me, an office for my dad, a dining room, a kitchen and the maid's room. It may also have had a parlor but I cannot recall. Perhaps the parlor was out of bounds for us. Some of our furniture from Germany arrived but not our toys, dolls, or other childhood treasures.

I grieved for my lost items from what now seemed a distant past. But then life went on.

CHAPTER SIXTEEN

LIFE IN FLORENCE

My sister and I were enrolled in a German school in Florence. It was a very long way from our apartment and required a journey by streetcar that included a transfer. We set out in the morning together and came back in the late afternoon together. Lunch was eaten at school under the watchful eyes of the staff. Table manners were strict.

The food itself was ghastly. The macaroni was mushy, the rice was gelatinous and soggy, and the atmosphere was frigid. The school itself however was a good one and had an ambitious curriculum.

We studied, French with a Frenchwoman, Italian with a Signorina Bicchierai who also taught embroidery, and English with a British miss. Besides that we studied geography, arithmetic, botany, gardening, art, music, and gymnastics. We even put on a play, *A Midsummer Night's Dream*. (I played the wall.)

Gradually life in Florence settled into a daily routine, but one vastly different from anything we had known before. There was the life of the street where we lived outside the *Porta Romana*, one of the old gates to the city. In the mornings we purchased our foodstuffs in the shops: jam in little papers rolled up at the corner and shoveled out of a big barrel, pasta strips in long white paper from a large drawer full of pasta, bread fresh from the bakery and butter and eggs from the creamery, all the while smelling the heat rising from the newly hosed down pavement where the voices of the housewives mingled melodiously with the shouting and laughing of children.

Sometimes I went to a well up the street to draw our water. This was located in a courtyard, and the courtyard itself felt cool and damp even on the hottest days. One had to lower a pail into the well to pull up the water and then put the water into bottles to carry home—a very different experience from Germany.

Or I would go up the street to fetch milk, fresh from the cow and still warm and frothy and full of cream that settled gently at the top of bowl.

On Saturday morning in the piazza down the street the farmers came with their produce: mountains of freshly picked pale golden grapes, still warm from the sun in their leaf-lined baskets, watermelons fragrant from the exposure to the warm rays of the sun, cantaloupes, figs (oh those figs, golden globes oozing their grainy brown seeds and sweeter than brown sugar) in addition to zucchini, lettuce and fragrant carrots still touched with the remnants of the earth.

In the summer the piazza would be turned into an outdoor theater where opera was performed on an outdoor stage, while we all sat on makeshift benches or stood about enchanted by the warm night, the lovely voices, and the beautiful costumes.

Often I went to the park with the neighborhood children, and there we climbed trees, and rolled down the green lawns. We played endless games that featured the saints and their blameless lives. And we collected violets that grew wild in the shade.

Gradually in Florence I changed from being a quiet little German girl into someone who was bolder and more adventurous. The sun shone daily and the air was warm and heavy with the smell of orange blossoms, roses, and the bay leaves of the hedges that surrounded neighboring houses. Before long I came to love Florence, my new friends, and my new life.

But things were not going well for my father, who, through no choice of his own was spending even more time at home now instead of working. Initially he had tried to sell some of the merchandise he had saved, but the Swiss and the Dutch did not want a German Jew to dispose of anything for fear of antagonizing the German government. And Italy still would not let him work.

So as I grew happier and happier with my new life my father was becoming more depressed. He went to the stock market with my uncle Erwin in order to get out of the house. He and other refugees went to the cafes and discussed politics and the general derailment of their lives.

We became friends with a painter, Meta Cohn-Handel (her fiancé was killed in the First World War and she was allowed the use of his name) who lived with her mother near us. Meta was always full of energy and immersed in some new project or other in her studio. We met a doctor and a pharmacist who had become refugees like us - waiting to go somewhere. We met a businessman with a wife and two daughters also waiting to leave for a new country that would accept them.

The younger of these two daughters was 14 when she met a handsome Italian boy of eighteen. Someone saw them kissing and reported it to her parents.

The precocious romance continued all the way to their journey to Cuba in search of a new life and from there to Los Angeles where they finally settled.

The girl, Renate grew into a lovely woman. The boyfriend Fausto studied engineering in Texas and came to Los Angeles by car on weekends. They eventually married and happily raised four children in Los Angeles.

As for us, despite all the pleasantness and hospitality of Florence, we were still without relatives there except for my aunt and uncle, and without longtime friends. And since we had no work or prospects for work, restructuring our lives became essential.

But because Florence was so beautiful and situated in the heart of the lovely Tuscan country, excursions to surrounding areas became delightful distractions. We bicycled most places. We'd pack a picnic of bread, cheese and fruit and visit the countryside. Sometimes we bought fruit and vegetables from the farmers; other times we just found a grassy spot where we could unpack and eat and rest before returning home.

One of our maids, Maria, a wonderfully outgoing girl with black hair and eyes and handsome features invited us to her home in the country. They were farmers. It was a large family with many children, some married and living at home. They cooked in front of an open hearth in huge metal pots.

My most vivid recollection of visiting them is sitting at a long table filled with food, everyone talking and laughing at once, and of later falling asleep in a huge bed. We all slept in the bed, my mother and father and sister and me. They had given us their bed-their generosity was huge. We bicycled back the next day, with their warmth and friendliness carried in our hearts.

When the weather grew too cold for outdoor excursions, we visited the museums that dotted the city. I knew nothing about art and no one had ever explained to me what to look for in a painting. So we simply looked.

I found the subjects of many paintings lurid and unappealing and it puzzled me to see them called masterpieces. My taste ran to Venus rising from the sea, the three Graces, and the pictures of the Madonna with her baby and of cherubs.

We also looked at the statues. Here my favorite was Michelangelo's *David*. Some of the statues were part of the fountains that were everywhere in the city. The lovely interplay of the water, the splash of it, and the green tracings it left on the stone all added to beauty of these magnificent carved figures.

We visited the churches too. In their dark hushed interiors where the light shone through the mosaics of the scenes colored glass, I saw black- robed old women, their heads covered with black shawls, reciting their rosaries. Black clad priests moved about quietly, murmuring to each other. They were on their own ground.

Inside these churches nuns wore voluminous habits, replete with wonderful elaborate head dresses starched to perfection. In their floor-length religious garments these nuns would appear to be gliding along the stone pavement inside the church, one that was beautifully inlaid with intricate patterns. A smell of incense settled gently in the air. Here it was cool and utterly peaceful.

I admired the offerings of gold objects and candles, and of flowers long faded. When told to look at the paintings on the walls I did, but what I loved most about the churches was the feeling of restrained drama: the priests hearing confession, the young girls in their white dresses at Communion, the baptismal font where each newcomer dipped and then made the sign of the cross.

I longed to participate, to belong to that established order. I read about the lives of the saints in garish comics. I too wanted to be a saint with a deep suffering that everyone admired me for, to be burned at the stake or buried alive or thrown to the lions. But in spite of the appeal of Catholicism as practiced there, I knew that I was Jewish and that none of it belonged to me.

We settled in at school. We diligently learned our lessons. I struggled valiantly to master the intricacies of watercolors, which unfortunately ran into each other to produce a muddied result. I tried to learn to knit, crotchet, and embroider as taught by a teacher I greatly admired, Signorina Bicchierai. These efforts of mine produced sweaty hands but not much else.

My worst nemesis was singing. I loved the sound of singing, however the singing teacher gently told me to:"Just move the lips, but don't sing."

The director of the school was German and taught a class in German literature. When I gave an incorrect answer he rapped me on the temples or the forehead with his knuckles to emphasize his irritation with me.

There was another Jewish girl in the school named Eva. She was lively with black hair and black eyes and was full of fun. She loved opera, particularly Mozart and especially *Le Nozze di Figaro* which she had memorized.

Another Jewish student was a shy, thin red haired girl named Sabine. Her pale freckled face rarely changed expression. Both girls left without our ever knowing why.

When my grandmother Adele next came for a visit she stayed at a new *pensione*. This one was run by a Jewish family from Berlin whose name was Schlesinger. There were two children, a boy named Thomas, and a baby that we called *Bebeli*. I cannot remember if it was also a boy. However Thomas was a little older than I was and proved a wonderful playmate for me. The two of us escaped from the ever worried grownups and their tense sad faces by playing Indians.

The *pensione* was in a converted villa surrounded by a huge garden. There were large pine trees whose cones were filled with *pignoli* to eat, bamboo to use for bows and arrows, overgrown paths to explore and weed- grown, open patches to build camp. I had never heard of James Fennimore Cooper before but now I lived the adventures from his stories. We were allowed to go to the store by ourselves and wonder of wonders I tried my very first soft drink and candy bar.

Of course this was strictly against what I knew to be parental wishes, making it all the more special to me. I can still recall the heat of the summer, the smell of the bamboo, the sticky drink and the glorious feeling of being alive and off on a real adventure.

It could not have lasted long, a month perhaps until my grandmother left. Near the end of her stay on a warm summer night as dusk was falling and we, Thomas and I were standing in the garden he leaned over and kissed me on the cheek. He said nothing and I said nothing.

Eventually we went into the house to join the adults. It was my very first enormously exciting adventure into uncharted territory. Unfortunately and unwisely I confided the enormity of it to my little sister. Consumed with jealousy and envy of my new friend and feeling left out, she told my parents. I submitted to their lectures; I learned this was not proper behavior. I never saw my friend Thomas again. I have often wondered about him.

CHAPTER SEVENTEEN

ENJOYING FLORENCE

By now we had become more settled immigrants to Italy. Living in Florence was no longer new or strange to us; it felt routine. We spoke Italian. We went to American movies where the actors spoke in Italian. All the little girls in the park wore their hair in curls like Shirley Temple and practiced tap dancing. We read Mickey Mouse books in Italian and celebrated Easter by going to the piazza and watching a dove, moved along a long line above our heads, usher in the holiday.

We went to the *Cascine* near the Arno for the horse races and the fairs. We came home with crickets in little wooden cages and listened to them sing. We had turtles that grew large and were released into the front garden where they grew larger still. We occasionally saw them scampering about awkwardly. We lay on our backs on hot summer days, in the empty lot next door and watched the shapes of the clouds as they scurried across the sky.

My parents, having settled in more slowly, cautiously began making longer term plans. Our German school was expensive. Italian schools were free and our Italian was now judged adequate. There was no problem for my sister Susi; she would be enrolled in a corresponding grade in grammar school. It was suggested to my parents that I try for enrollment in the teacher preparatory school, called *Scuola Magistrale*, one Mussolini had established in order to have teachers to change the largely illiterate population into an educated one.

In order to be selected to attend *Scuola Magistrale* however, one had to pass an extensive written and oral examination that covered history, geography, Italian language, grammar, usage, poetry, some art history, math, and science. We had to memorize certain poems and recite them for the examiners.

My parents, on the advice of friends, hired an Italian woman as a tutor. She lived in an apartment some distance by streetcar and was probably a former teacher, now in her fifties. She was very strict and businesslike but in spite of that she communicated to me her intense love of the language and an appreciation of the delight in its poetry. I worked extremely hard at mastering all of the knowledge required for the entire summer of my eleventh year. I took the exam, and came in third citywide. When I saw the posted list at the school I was indeed very proud of myself. I'd come a long way from my shaky start as a clumsy, inky-fingered first grader in Pforzheim!

CHAPTER EIGHTEEN

SCHOOL AND OTHER FUN

Now began an enchanted period of my life. I loved the *Scuola Magistrale*. I loved the teachers. I loved my fellow students. I became truly excited about learning for the first time, in the way I still am today. And for the first time I began to feel that I fit in. I was not Italian, I had an accent, I was not Catholic but my fellow students and I had common interests in literature and ideas.

My main teacher was Signorina Gina de Meo. She had black hair, fair skin, huge black eyes framed by long lashes, a lovely figure, and at the throat of her black uniform, she wore chiffon scarves of pale lilac and other soft colors. She was in her twenties and had a soft lovely voice and a charming smile. I was totally smitten. I longed for her approval and worked hard for it. She in turn was very sweet and patient with me and generous with her praise. The other teachers were encouraging as well with all the students. Even the singing teacher made me feel wanted and teachable. The math teacher was friendly and helpful. Since it was a girls' school and we all were required to wear identical black cotton uniforms and black shoes; it was egalitarian.

My best friend, Leda Landini and I walked to school together every day. Her mother had died and her father was a pharmacist. She wore long beautiful blonde braids to her willowy waist and loved school as much as I did. We discussed everything. I felt that my life had been transformed in an unimaginably wonderful way. We were sponges that absorbed the kindness and the interest of these young dedicated women teachers and in turned they filled our minds and hearts with the magic of a classical education. We studied Latin, and Dante Alighieri, the ancient Greeks and Italian history with an absorption that was total. I hardly paid attention to life outside school.

But even in this enchanting situation, changes were occurring in the outside world that would intrude on my new happiness.

Hitler had joined forces with Mussolini. They had become allies. The first impact of this was that joining a particular Italian Youth organization became mandatory at school. So I joined the *Ballila*. My mother bought me the uniform which consisted of a black shirt, white blouse, black stockings and shoes and a very fetching black cape on which I soon sewed red stripes I had earned practicing drilling.

I became a squad leader and had a group of young girls to drill. It was fun. I was promoted. It must have been the German blood in my veins. My parents became alarmed and uncertain about it.

In the summers we escaped the heat of the city and generally rented accommodations in the mountains or at the beach. One summer while my dad was traveling trying to turn merchandise into a living my mother and Sue and I spent the time in a small rented room at the beach.

I cannot recall how long a sojourn we had there. But I do remember the cool mornings and the soft air, the hot sand and the stifling heat. My mother was tired and irritable and the small room we rented was crowded with all three of us. We bought fruits and some cheese and that was all we ate together with some crusty bread. Susi and I never asked questions or commented on what we experienced but played our games, quarreled over small matters, and like children everywhere, waited for time to pass.

That was a limbo of sorts; both better and worse things lay ahead.

CHAPTER NINETEEN

SUMMER IN *ALLEGHE*

Another summer we went to a small resort called *Alleghe*. It was located in the mountains and we had a cabin on a lake that was about two to three miles across, or so it seemed to my childish eyes. The cabin we rented said W. C. which my parents believed meant water closet, or toilet rather than outhouse which their German upbringing could not easily accommodate for long.

What it meant in this instance was a trough, with two raised metal platforms for the feet, set about a foot and a half apart on which one squatted, proceeded to do one's business and then, flushed with a water closet attached to the wall. Not what my parents had in mind and dreadfully difficult for my grandmother, who had grown nearly blind with glaucoma by the time she stayed with us briefly then.

The cabin bordered the lake. Along the sides of it there were rows of beans and peas, tomato plants and radishes. We could harvest what we needed. I remember the sweetness of the fresh peas, still warm from the sun, green and delicate in their little green beds. I also loved picking the green beans as they climbed up the poles, little soldiers in a row.

We hiked in the surrounding woods and picked mushrooms. My father having grown up in the forest was experienced at telling the poisonous ones from the edible ones. We always double checked with him. We picked wild strawberries and raspberries and bowls and bowls of blueberries. Our supper consisted of fruit and milk and a piece of bread and butter.

I was allowed to take the wooden rowboat with its two wooden oars across the lake to the hotel where my grandmother Adele stayed. I loved rowing quietly across the small lake feeling the sun on my skin and smelling the cool water. Near the shore there were great balls of water snakes clearly visible in the water.

These added an element of danger that I also liked, and that kept my sister from joining my excursions. When I had difficulty falling asleep during my later life I recalled the lake, the old rowboat with its clumsy wooden oars in their rusty attachments, the quiet peace and gentle sound of the water rippling and above all the smells of the mountains: fir trees, pine needles, a musty sharp smell mixed with the sound of the birds and the crickets.

I was free in my solitude that summer; and I was growing up.

When my grandmother Adele left *Alleghe* she went to join my aunt Ilse and her husband and children who were staying in the Austrian Alps. She had hired a taxi for all of us to cross the Alps at sunrise from Italy to Austria.

It was dark when we arose - dark and cold. I felt cross. We huddled into the cold taxi crowding against each other for heat. We began the ascent. Soon Sue was complaining of car sickness.

The narrow road wound up and up. Then the sun began to rise in the sky. The snow that never melted at that altitude began to look faintly pink. The pink became deeper and gradually turned to peach. It was dazzling! Then the sun, having risen, turned the snow to white crystal everywhere.

The magic of sunrise has stayed with me all my life. When I get up in the early morning and watch the eastern sky turn softly rose, I still think of that trip though the Alps with my parents, grandmother and sister.

The summer passed quickly.

We returned to the city of Florence.

CHAPTER TWENTY

TROUBLE HEATING UP

In school once again we were informed Hitler was coming to visit Florence and that one student, based on merit would be chosen to present a bouquet to him!

Of all possible students, I was chosen! My mother discreetly informed them it was not a suitable choice.

I felt relieved about that but now I started re-experiencing all the old tensions from Germany and elsewhere. Who was I? Where, if anywhere did I belong? What would become of my family, spread not just throughout Europe now but over two or three continents?

Around then my father left Florence as a precaution. Aunt Ilse, Uncle Erwin, Walter and Ann had already left for the United States shortly before that. We had a long sad goodbye with my grandmothers. At the time Aunt Tala was nursing her husband Sepp through his last illness in Pforzheim.

My father was deeply saddened to part from his brother, my Uncle Erwin. My mother was equally sad to say goodbye to her sister, my Aunt Ilse. Both grandmothers felt they would never see their children again. We had a last photograph taken by a German refugee in Florence of all of us, sober, unsmiling.

My grandmother Adele returned to Hamburg, while my grandmother Helene stayed with us. My father had gone away on a business trip in anticipation of Hitler's visit to Italy.

But as it turned out, his absence did not keep the police from our door.

◆

We are asleep in our beds when the pounding on the heavy wooden door sounds. It is about two a.m. My mother gets up and asks who it is. "It's the police! Open up!"

When my mother asks what they want they tell her "Get dressed!" They want to take her to jail!

My mother suddenly turns into a lioness before our eyes. "I will not leave my small children alone with their blind grandmother," she screams at them. "My husband is out of town and I am alone."

She opens the door to a small, previously unused porch in the front of the apartment. She stands on this porch and screams for help. The neighbors emerge and begin to take part in the drama. My sister and I cry. We have not been this terrified since leaving Germany on the train where my parents had been searched.

My grandmother, who does not understand a word of Italian, becomes alarmed.

"HELP, HELP!" cries my mother.

"Brava, Brava!" shout the neighboring women.

"Mamma, Mamma!' cry my sister and I.

All is tears, shouts, and chaos.

It is too much for the Italian police. They do not break the door down after all.

They do not shoot through the lock, either. My everlasting gratitude goes to the Italian gendarmes. They sit and wait outside our door until morning.

In the morning after a sleepless night my mother tells me," You must go for the lawyer. He lives around the corner and up the street. Tell him it is an emergency and bring him back with you."

Heart pounding, I open the door and look out. I see two Italian carabinieri in full regalia, their guns drawn and pointed at me.

I tell them I am going for the lawyer. I close the door behind me and hold my breath. No one shoots me.

I run down the stairs and up the street to the lawyer and return with him. My mother never leaves us.

The lawyer leaves, returns a short while later, and says they had wanted my aunt Ilse, not my mother, for reasons we never learn.

But life in beautiful pleasant Florence feels different after that. From now on we are always on the alert for the unexpected knock at the door from someone in uniform who wants one of us this time.

Soon it will be necessary to leave here just as we had to leave Germany.

And soon Hitler himself will be here in Florence with his new ally, Mussolini. Such is life on the run.

Florence has been kind to us up to now, but . . .

✦

Hitler came to Florence. I went down into the street and watched the parade. The cheering of the crowd was deafening. Everyone was shouting. He was surrounded by uniformed SS.

All this was terribly frightening for a small Jewish girl. I ran home. The sounds of the jubilant crowd's cheering rang in my ears. Mussolini and Hitler rode together down a major street in Florence. Their pact concluded they were now joined in a treaty that meant death for Jews in Italy.

Our period of refuge there was over.

We knew we had to move on.

My father returned from his trip and learned of my mother's encounter with the Italian police and of the current political climate. We again made plans to pack.

I could not return to my beloved school, my friends, my studies, my hard-won place in my happy little universe.

It felt like death, again. *Run! Run! Hitler's coming!*

CHAPTER TWENTY-ONE

LAST GLIMPSES OF ITALY

My father decided to join his brother Erwin in San Francisco as soon as our visas arrived. Erwin had found a sponsor for us, someone who would guarantee that we would not become a burden to the country. We took physical examinations and were judged healthy. We were immunized. We booked passage on the *Rex*, a large passenger liner from Genoa to New York, and then on a smaller ship, the *City of Norfolk* that would take us through the Panama Canal from New York to San Francisco.

Before we left here forever though, my father wanted to see Naples and Pompeii and especially the Vesuvius volcano.

I remember it was hot on that trip. My little sister grew uncomfortable and cried. My mother was tense and upset at leaving her family, especially her mother and brothers behind in Germany. No one wanted to leave here, and now we would be leaving not just Germany but Europe for a whole unknown continent.

But when we finally reached Pompeii and saw the mountain, with its crown of smoke curling into the pure blue sky, I grew excited despite the family mood. My father had rented a taxi to take us up the curving path to the top of Vesuvius.

My sister became carsick and my mother looked as though she might join her. Only my father and I remained game for this new adventure.

Finally the cab stopped. The driver would go no further. My mother and sister refused to leave the cab. My father and I began to climb until we reached an open area where small rivulets of red hot molten lava snaked down the rocky terrain. We jumped over a couple of very narrow ones.

Oh, the adventure of it! The mountain emitted a thunderous noise that was frightening but with my tall daddy by my side I had no feeling of danger. It was an unforgettable experience for me.

When we returned to Florence our visas had arrived. We began to pack. My mother had clothes made for us and shoes in order to use up money we could not take with us.

I began to plan on what book to take for the long trip and decided on *I Promessi Sposi*. I was more comfortable with Italian than with German at this time and I was beginning to be interested in romance, which this book contained. It was the adventure of a couple who had been betrothed but whose marriage had been prevented for a large number of pages of beautiful Italian story telling.

To the extent he could under the circumstances my father looked forward to San Francisco. He had seen pictures of the Golden Gate Bridge when it was completed and was photographed in the Italian newspaper and he had shown it to me. It seemed magical.

For my part, I was more interested in the abdication of the King of England for the woman he loved, which most of the Italian girls my age were discussing avidly that summer.

One day it was time to go. Because it was summer vacation I could not say goodbye to my friends or my teachers. I always felt a terrible sorrow about not saying farewell. I had never before realized what an important function we fulfill by saying goodbye.

We took the train to Genoa and there boarded the *Rex* which was waiting for us at the dock.

And that ended our stay in Florence, in many ways the happiest time of my life so far.

CHAPTER TWENTY-TWO

BOUND FOR AMERICA

The *Rex* at that time was the third largest ocean liner that made the trip across the Atlantic. It was enormous to my childish eyes. There were three classes of passengers aboard, the most expensive first class passage, the less pricey second class and finally our class which was third or tourist class. Absolutely no contact occurred among the classes. We never caught a glimpse of each other.

Each separate class had its own facilities, dining rooms, swimming pools, and entertainment. We'd been told it was most fun in tourist because the elderly occupied the other two but I could not tell.

Our cabin was small for the four of us, but the bunk beds proved a delightful novelty. I was allowed the top bunk. My sister and I were also free to roam the ship (our portion of it) to our heart's content.

I immediately talked to all the Italian crew members and found them fun and friendly. We had a children's area replete with a trained supervisor who devised games and competitions for us together with prizes. There were books and puzzles and sports equipment and on warm days we had the swimming pool.

Many adults aboard were in a mood to chat-unusual among adults in my experience. However when my parents saw me becoming friendly they quickly told me to be very careful about strangers.

The meals were glorious. Menus for each meal were beautifully engraved, elaborate affairs that changed every day for every meal.

First there would be early tea. This was available in the cabin from a steward but not suitable for us. Then there was breakfast which we could partake of by ourselves and order what we liked from the menu. The waiters always had something special for us.

Under the door of our cabin would be messages in the mornings and sometimes during the day that announced news events; special areas we were traversing, mileage information, weather, and special events for us. Then at eleven we had broth on the deck chairs where the steward brought us blankets to keep out the chill.

I felt incredibly adult sipping my broth and talking with other passengers in Italian or in German. There were many other refugees on the ship. All were cautious about talking to strangers at first, but then some of us got to know each other.

Lunch was mostly sandwiches or light meals for the children eaten in the children's area. Since I had my sister along, we formed the nucleus of a team and usually were joined by another little girl close to our age.

Dinner meant dressing up. My father and mother looked resplendent in clothes we seldom saw them wearing. They danced and enjoyed a respite from their careworn days. I too danced with my father who was accomplished at the waltz and the foxtrot.

One time during a wonderful dinner, the ship swayed strongly and unexpectedly. My father had been talking right then, and a fishbone got stuck in his throat. He was rushed to the ship's doctor who extracted the bone with dexterity. My father became a celebrity among the passengers who wanted to know about the medical facilities.

Soon the journey was over. I remember going on deck as we steamed into New York Harbor. We saw the Statue of Liberty holding her torch aloft. I looked around me to see the passengers sobbing, tears streaming down their faces. My father was wiping his glasses, his nose pinched and red. I too felt my eyes mist; it was catching, this feeling we were sharing.

I have never forgotten my first view of the Statue of Liberty. Years later when I steamed into New York Harbor on a vacation trip I made with my husband, my eyes began to fill with tears again as I recalled to Sam the memory of my first glimpse of America, all those years ago.

CHAPTER TWENTY-THREE

ARRIVAL IN NEW YORK

New York! We disembarked from the huge ship and like international passengers anywhere, we were handed right over to customs.

Naturally after so many earlier, less than pleasant experiences at various borders, we felt apprehensive. So we were unprepared for the polite, casual reception we received. America's customs officers simply waved us through, unconcerned about us or our belongings.

Now however, there came a new completely unexpected difficulty. To descend from the area where we had disembarked to the level of the city of New York one had to take the escalator down. None of us had ever seen an escalator before and both my mother and my sister refused to get on it. Understandably both had been through many upsetting experiences and this evidently was the final straw!

My father became totally distraught. Eventually he took hold of my mother and managed to get her down and then carried my sister, weeping bitterly, to street level. A taxi took us to a hotel.

Taking my first car ride in America, I could not believe how new everything looked compared to any European city I had ever known.

I was awed by the tall buildings and the strangeness of the people. They were dressed differently, and they had a busy, hurried look quite unlike any I had ever seen.

From our new hotel my parents called relatives and we went to visit them in their New York apartment. I remember that as being small and rather dark.

I vaguely remember dinner and conversation but both my sister and I were exhausted from the day. We fell asleep.

My parents could not wake us. So they left us with their relatives. In the middle of the night my sister woke up and upon finding herself in a totally strange place without my parents promptly had hysterics.

I woke up and tried to figure out what was happening. I was twelve and used to looking after both of us. We made a careful inspection of the premises and saw no note from my parents. We knew our relatives' name: Heinz Mueller, but nothing else.

My parents were somewhere in this strange city but we could not remember where. We could not reach them. We decided to sit quietly and wait for daybreak. Eventually we both fell asleep again.

We had lived through our first day in America.

Soon enough though, we would learn that our new homeland would offer us all kinds of other surprises.

CHAPTER TWENTY-FOUR

ON TO SAN FRANCISCO

Within a day or two we embarked again for our ultimate destination in America: San Francisco. The ship we took now was the smaller *City of Norfolk*, smaller because we would be sailing on her through the Panama Canal.

My father loved the idea of the journey and was interested in seeing everything along the way. He also felt that we, especially he and my mother needed a break from the sadness of the goodbyes and all the anxieties we'd had before our departure. A sea voyage paid for with moneys that could not be exported was his brilliant solution.

While the *Rex* had been a huge city at sea, the *City of Norfolk* was a small, cozy village. It was easy to make friends and though everyone still dressed for dinner the general feeling was far less formal.

We met a charming woman named Celia Jaffer and her daughter Frances. Celia had recently been widowed and her daughter was seventeen or eighteen and just starting Stanford University. She was about five years older than me. I was enchanted by both of them, and by their continuing kindness and interest in us and by their familiarity with the strange new world we had just entered.

Celia was slim and beautifully groomed with long legs clad in lovely nylons and delicious high heeled pumps. She spoke English in a low husky voice. Her recent loss of her husband and her inheritance of his business all made her unusual and exotic in my eyes.

She enjoyed my father's business experience and common sense and obvious interest in her. My father though faithful at all times to my mother to the best of my knowledge had been a bachelor until he mid thirties and was a charmer when he wanted to be. He was also a salesman, eventually selling her a beautiful pin consisting of a wreath of flowers each made of different precious stones with the leaves of emeralds.

Frances interested me because she too differed from any of my former acquaintances. For her graduation her mother had given her a short jacket of leopard fur which she wore with a fitted skirt that set off her lovely figure. She appeared to be far more independent from her mother than any young woman I knew. Celia and Frances both tried to prepare me for the coming culture shock.

Our trip through the Panama Canal in August of 1938 was very hot. I remember seeing my very first pelican sitting on a wooden pole protruding from the water. The brilliant green jungle vegetation lined the shore and appeared to steam up in the oppressive hot weather.

The ship moved slowly through the locks, which fascinated my father. Soon we were in the Pacific Ocean and had left the Atlantic behind us.

My parents did not allow us to visit the cities on the shore. Possibly they had been warned of disease. They themselves went ashore in Acapulco and were surprised that there were open sewers. The heat was overwhelming and they returned quickly.

Our journey ended on Labor Day when we entered San Francisco Harbor. That day was lovely, cool, sunny, and breezy. We moved under the Golden Gate Bridge, the same one I had seen pictures of in an Italian newspaper once its construction was complete.

And then we disembarked, welcomed at long last by my aunt Ilse, my uncle Erwin and my cousins, Walter and Ann.

Thus began the hardest of my new beginnings.

But on that day we were simply glad to be alive and to have safely arrived, and that some if not all of our family members were being reunited.

I was not yet thirteen but it felt to me that day as if I had lived many more years.

CHAPTER TWENTY-FIVE

CULTURE SHOCK IN SAN FRANCISCO

Noone who greeted us in San Francisco looked the way I remembered them. Aunt Ilse appeared thin and ill; Uncle Erwin serious and tired. Cousin Walter my former playmate looked much older than I remembered, and thinner and more distracted. And Cousin Ann was no longer the cuddly toddler I remembered; she had turned into a quiet, sturdy six year old.

Life had clearly worn on all of them.

Still my father was overjoyed to see his dearly loved brother and my mother delighted to see her only sister again. My aunt and uncle had rented us a furnished apartment on 9th Avenue in the Richmond district in San Francisco.

A friend of Erwin's who owned a Buick picked up our luggage and we all climbed in somehow and drove to our new apartment. I had no idea what to expect but hoped for the best.

That hope was short-lived. The place was up three or four flights of dark and malodorous stairs. The carpet or what there was of it, appeared dark and dirty. Our windows looked out upon an alley and did not allow in much light. The bathroom was cramped, damp and dingy.

The kitchen was dismal. It was awful. Erwin apologized saying there was not much in the way of furnished places and they were all very expensive. After our furniture was shipped we could find something better. No one said much. No one needed to.

When I went downtown for the first time with my Dad I saw that Uncle Erwin had rented a very small cubicle in the back of a jewelry store owned by a Mr. Kahn. The store became their base of operations. They established contacts with wholesalers. They made the decision to go into the wholesale diamond business. It was a field they both knew well.

I am not certain if my father had any merchandize left from his factory, but probably not because he had used it to finance our last few years and our trip.

Erwin, who was younger and both more adventurous and more outgoing had made contacts everywhere with his charm and good looks and his thorough knowledge of the jewelry business. We were truly fortunate to have him laying the groundwork for our arrival.

My father was almost fifty years old when we arrived. He had to become far more proficient in English, establish himself in a new business, meet and sell to new customers, learn the customs in the new country, learn the streets, the streetcars, and find all the typical support systems: doctors, lawyers, accountants, bankers.

One of his first acts was typical. He and my mother enrolled in night school to learn English and American history and institutions in order to become citizens.

My mother was more proficient in English than my father. She had had an English governess as a youngster and was gifted in languages. Both my mother and Aunt Ilse found the language less of a handicap than did my father and uncle; however they were not trying to sell anything.

They had far different concerns. The money they were given to live on was very limited. The brothers needed every penny to put into the new business. My mother, who had never managed without a maid was now caring for four people without help. She had to shop carefully to stretch every penny. She had to learn to do heavy cleaning with new products previously unknown to her. She had to wash and iron. She had to enroll us in school.

And my mother needed to stay level-headed in spite of my father's anxiety and frequent depression. There was not much to be cheery about. Life in our new country was unrelenting hard work for both of them.

I escaped the only way I knew. Next door to us on 9th Avenue was a public library. It was the first one I had ever encountered in my entire life. I could not believe my good fortune. Free books! With a library card we could take out six books at a time!

First I read all the Italian books on the shelves. Then I read all the German books. The foreign language books were limited to perhaps twenty or so. Then gradually I tried English, first fairy tales that I already knew, and gradually other books.

I loved to sit in the pleasant airy library and read, away from our hideous apartment, my sad and troubled parents, and my difficult days in school. It had been decided I was to repeat the sixth grade in order to polish my English language skills and familiarize myself with the new customs.

That was hard. I already felt older than my years because of all we'd experienced; but now I would be behind my peers in school.

CHAPTER TWENTY-SIX

SAN FRANCISCO SCHOOL DAYS

I was enrolled in the sixth grade at Sutro Grammar School and my teacher was a corpulent heavily corseted lady named Miss O'Leary. She immediately singled me out and made me stand in front of the class and tell the rest of the students where I had come from. The general response was, "Say something in Italian!"

This was not easy. I never knew what they wanted me to say and they would not tell me when I asked but generally said, "Oh, anything" or "I don't know." Gradually I developed a repertoire of, "I like being in America" (which was not true, I hated it and was dreadfully homesick for my beautiful Florence, my beloved Signorina De Meo, and my school friend, Leda Landini).

There was no turning back. I knew it, although I sometimes pretended turning back might be possible. I would turn on the Italian hour on the radio. San Francisco had a large Italian population and there were programs in that language. My father would not allow that if he was home. We had to learn English and increase our proficiency he insisted; and he was busy doing just that.

My first friend in school was of Italian descent, Gloria Di Salvo. She belonged to a large noisy Italian family, was dark haired and dark eyed and though we had very little in common we walked back and forth to school together.

After the first semester at Sutro I was enrolled in Presidio Junior High. By this time our furniture had arrived and we moved to Seventeenth Avenue in the Richmond district. My new school was on Twenty Eighth Avenue.

Every morning Gloria and I walked along Clement Street and exchanged the sort of information girls valued in those days. Movie stars, boys in school, other girls, and teachers were the usual topics. This was a far cry from what I was used to discussing with Leda-philosophy, religious views and Dante.

During those first weeks and months in America I had a feeling of having only part of myself present. But I was advanced a grade now that my English had improved sufficiently.

Still, the language gave me surprising difficulties sometimes. For instance we had French as an elective, and one day I stood up to translate and forgot which language was French since they were about equally familiar. I read the French thinking it was English. The class laughed, and I felt embarrassed.

And there were other things new and baffling about American life—the kinds uniquely, often painfully important to teenagers.

First there was the hair. In Italy we washed it, parted it, and put a barrette in it to hold it back from our face. In San Francisco hair was an altogether different matter. It had to be waved and properly curled, preferably in a pompadour in front and drawn back on the sides. The back fell in soft long cascades, except that my own hair refused to cooperate. It was brown, very soft, wavy and wispy. I slept in curlers, but the damp San Francisco air dissolved all curl by the time I'd walked the first block to school. Only in the short summer months could I keep my hair properly waved!

The next difficulty was my European clothes. My parents had spent the money we could not take out of Italy on buying us clothes, made to order by a seamstress, and shoes.

Our clothes immediately marked us as "different". The other girls wore skirts and sweaters and saddle shoes. I desperately wanted a skirt and sweater!

That first winter, my mother worked for a general's wife helping her serve at dinner parties. She also worked as a practical nurse very briefly. It was tremendously disturbing to my father that his wife would have to resort to this, but my mother wanted spending money.

I frequently voiced my deep desire for a sweater. In my mind's eye I saw a pure white, softly formfitting, hip length long sleeved cashmere sweater.

When I opened my Christmas gift on our first real American Christmas my mother had indeed bought me a sweater. But it was an unfortunate blue gray, ribbed, short sleeved, buttoned, waist long cardigan that made me look as though I was wearing my grandmother's hand-me-down.

I could not weep or even complain-my mother had tried so hard to please me! But she had no inkling what fashionable schoolgirls wore in America. I choked out a thank you but wore the awful sweater only to the movies-under a coat!

Clothes remained a problem since money was very scarce. My father worked hard all day trying to establish a clientele among the San Francisco jewelers. He had no car and walked or took the street car to make sales calls. At night he and my mother still attended night school for English and American history for their citizenship requirements.

And my mother still did all the housework, washing, cleaning and cooking without any help, human or machine. She shopped and carried the groceries home by street car and by walking, often traveling far for bargains.

The washing was hung on a line over our landlady's yard with clothes pins; and with a strong wind, not uncommon in San Francisco it would blow off and then needed locating and retrieving from the various neighbors.

My sister and I wanted to look like our classmates. My mother especially felt our pressure on her to buy us what other girls our age wore. However she also relied on her own upbringing and memories of life abroad in choosing our outfits. No formfitting sweaters that showed the bust line, no tight skirts, no clunky jewelry were allowed. When added to the lack of funds that left us looking dowdy.

I finally convinced her to buy me a pretty light blue fitted wool suit with silver buttons and a slightly flared skirt. I loved it!

But soon, too soon, my figure began to change. I was turning 14, and I rapidly outgrew my beloved outfit.

At that age my lack of fashionable clothes remained a problem, although not my only one.

CHAPTER TWENTY-SEVEN

UNEASY ADOLESCENCE

In my mother's youth, middle class girls were expected to have certain skills. She exerted tremendous effort to duplicate these requirements in us despite our new location and limited finances. We joined the Jewish Center and my sister and I were soon enrolled in classes there for swimming, tap dancing, ballroom dancing, and social clubs.

We took the streetcar and earnestly put on our tap shoes, or for swimming lessons our hideous gray rented bathing suits, and gamely attended the classes. But we made little progress. We continued awkwardly and persistently.

On one occasion we forgot the money for the streetcar and my sister wept copiously until the conductor relented and let us ride for free. Another time at the pool, an aggressive older girl held my head under water until I felt myself drowning and with that realization, I fought myself free.

Eventually, when my father bought a house, we stopped attending. We were older and it was too far away from our new residence.

My mother also bought us tennis rackets. On Saturdays and Sundays we went to the public courts that were generally free (tennis was not popular then) and learned how to play. We were taught by our mother, not always the best idea. She had been a good tennis player and an enthusiastic one but I had not inherited her athletic zeal.

My personal preference ran to reading on weekends, but my mother would not brook any excuse for a lack of more vigorous activity. She also bought roller skates for me and I remember enjoying roller skating up and down the block with the other girls. The skates were awkward and required a key to tighten them to the shoes. They also made an incredible racket going down the street. The damp, misty San Francisco air made them rust and we outgrew them quickly.

On Saturdays we went to the "show". That meant the Saturday kids' matinee. It cost a dime and lasted from one to five in the afternoon. It started with the news, then the cartoons, then a continuing feature always ending with the girl under a train about to run over her or some other terrible imminent fate.

Then came the main features, an A movie and a B movie. We could take a candy bar from home (cheaper than in the show) or fruit. I loved the movies!

My favorite actor was Errol Flynn. Handsome, swashbuckling clad in wonderful tight fitting britches, he simply entranced me. My other favorite was Leslie Howard. He was remote and elegant. There was an air of distance about him I found appealing.

In the evening we listened to the radio. My father had his favorite shows headed by Eddie Cantor. Eventually he bought a better radio for himself and my sister and I inherited the old one. We listened to "The Shadow" and other mystery stories. We also listened to the "Hit Parade" on Saturday night much to the disgust of my father who called the music trash.

My father listened to the stock reports every morning at eight while eating breakfast and we were not allowed to make a sound. At night he listened to the news and once again we had to be absolutely quiet.

Sundays we visited with my aunt and uncle and played with our cousins, until the day came when my father bought a car. Thereafter we began driving into the surrounding mountains to hike and picnic. Sometimes we visited the farming areas and bought fruits and vegetables.

My dad missed terribly the countryside of his past and the mountains of his youth. He had always shed his troubles in the mountains and seemed younger and more energetic after a good hike or climb.

Here then, if the weather was splendid we enjoyed Golden Gate Park. Sue and I tried the slides, something not at all familiar to us. There were free concerts and museums to visit, along with the Arboretum, the Zoo and my father's favorite, Stern Grove for the Sunday concerts where we frequently met friends and picnicked.

I knew that all this was my father's and perhaps my mother's idea of an enjoyable Sunday but slowly I began to feel that I wanted to fill my time in other ways. This I could not express. It was unthinkable. I began missing my friends in Italy, though I knew it was impossible to ever return. I was homesick, though I did not know for what exactly, a way of life that suited me more, perhaps.

Meanwhile the news coming from Europe was increasingly disastrous. We began receiving pitiful letters from family and friends still trapped in Germany, and now feeling desperate to escape. My grandmother Adele had finally begun to understand that there was no choice but to leave-to stay in Germany meant certain death.

My uncle Werner was briefly imprisoned in a concentration camp but he was released after great effort on everyone's part. He escaped to England.

My uncle Gerhardt's wife had family in Denmark. One night he, his wife and their two children packed a few belongings and boarded a fishing boat in Hamburg at night and made the trip across the North Sea to Denmark.

My mother's cousin Alice had two children, Anneliese, the older, and a younger son, Hans. They also had a terrible choice to make: to send their beloved oldest child, their only daughter to America on a Save the Children program or perhaps watch her perish with the rest of the family.

They sent her to America. She found a Jewish family in New York that took her in, cared for her and enabled her to become a doctor. The rest of the family were able to save themselves and their son and emigrated to Sao Paolo, Brazil.

Eventually the family was reunited but the daughter always felt that the parents preferred their son, because they kept him, and the son always felt they preferred the daughter because her picture was everywhere and they talked about her so much.

Then there were those who could not escape: all my German aunts and uncles except my aunt Tala and my aunts Ilse and Gisela.

The news also increasingly mentioned the threat of war. My father and mother who read the newspapers and listened to the news on the radio became more certain with each passing week that war was inevitable in order to stop the murder of the Jews in Europe and the invasion of other countries by Germany.

One Sunday when we had parked at the Legion of Honor and looked out at the bay, the news of the attack on Pearl Harbor was announced. War was now inevitable.

My father looked at us, my sister and myself, and said:"Now I am deeply grateful you are girls and not boys and will never have to go to war."

CHAPTER TWENTY-EIGHT

COLLEGE DAYS

When I graduated from high school in 1942 my parents did not want to send me to college, figuring that any degree I earned would be wasted once I married. But I persisted in my desire to attend the University of California, Berkeley and finally they relented.

After my nomadic, uncertain youth I loved the whole college experience—my classes, my fellow students and the serious but not too solemn atmosphere. Finally I had arrived to somewhere where my thirst for learning was quenchable and where such thirst was a good thing—the right thing, in fact.

As a freshman I lived in a boarding house called Bonhaven. I roomed with a girl from Sacramento named Helen. She was a fresh air fiend, and she insisted on having the window wide open. I had allergies, so I spent most nights uncomfortable, coughing and sneezing.

Helen had been orphaned at a young age so she was extremely independent and somewhat pushy. I was 17 and this was my first time away from home, so I let her have her way. Subsequently I roomed with Shirley. Shirley and I had a nice relationship, and we became very good friends.

At first I cried a lot and was homesick, but gradually I got over it as my love of learning took over. Meanwhile though, there were various personality issues and sensitive feelings at my boarding house.

For instance my friend Jean felt we weren't getting enough fruits and vegetables to eat and the house mother responsible for food started to cry when Jean criticized the food. Eventually this was resolved and we all went back to eating like before, and the house mother stopped crying. Given all I had been through I was more flexible about daily living than most of my house mates.

One initial college subject I studied with enthusiasm was Spanish. My first goal was to study abroad as part of my college education and eventually teach English in South America where some of my German relatives now lived. Since I was by now used to traveling and spoke a lot of languages it seemed natural I would become a journalist or diplomat.

Meanwhile I explored other academic subjects and took many interesting electives. One of these was philosophy. This was a natural subject for me, and I especially loved the class discussions and the teacher.

To my surprise I also loved geology. I got an "A" in that subject, which shocked me. Much later in life, whenever my husband Sam and I went on a driving trip I would study the sides of the highways, determining the various rock strata, as I'd done long ago in that class.

In fact, one of our most memorable geological experiences came many decades after college, when Sam and I took a trip up to Mt. St. Helen's, in Washington State a short while after the famous volcanic eruption of 1980.

As I recall, the area was covered with ashes and resembled a desert. Still, we could see even then, peeking out from beneath the heavy ash, some timid green sprouts of new growth: testament to the abiding strength of life. We saw the first birds arriving back to their natural habitat, and the first rabbits and moles shyly reclaiming their territory.

I was deeply moved by these reminders, echoes from my youth, of how life springs back to normal again, against all odds.

Nearby at the Mount St. Helens National Volcanic Monument we watched a video that showed how even in the hot lava there are certain elements of life that regenerate; and we saw from that how magnificent the capacity to regenerate truly is, even from mere ashes.

At UC Berkeley I also studied English literature and took special delight in Shakespeare's plays. These seemed to explain so much about the world and human frailties in particular. I also took Latin, something I enjoyed immensely as a fluent Italian speaker and that served me well later in law school.

My first couple semesters were the best. My mind was like a thirsty sponge soaking up everything I could learn.

But life was also about to change in a way that was decidedly non-academic.

CHAPTER TWENTY-NINE

FALLING IN LOVE

One night my college roommates talked me into attending a dance for servicemen, and it was there that I met my future husband Sam.

My roommate Helen had forced me to go, although, as I protested, I didn't dance and wasn't interested. But the dance turned out to be a life-changing event.

The dance was held at the Student Union and was mainly for the servicemen enrolled at UC Berkeley, of which there were many at the time, Froli Cal dances they were called. I wore casual clothes— a summer skirt and moccasins and did not expect to meet my future husband that night.

But I did!

Sam was tall and fair-haired with green eyes. I was dumbfounded because he was cute and he was American, and he had actually asked me to dance! I let him know we had the same religion, something that would have been obvious from my old last name, Goldbaum, but not so obvious with my new last name Gordon.

We danced, and after awhile Sam asked me if I'd like to go for a Coke. I had never had a Coke (my German parents weren't ones to put soft drinks in the house and college life was still fairly new to me) but I said okay.

When we got to the Coke machine Sam confessed he didn't have a nickel so I bought my own Coke. That was our first date.

As I got to know Sam better we discovered we had many shared interests. Like me, Sam was interested in poetry and Shakespeare, and he liked reading. He also played violin and had done some composing. He walked me home to my boarding house and soon we were exchanging information that was fairly intimate.

But since I lived in a boarding house and he was in the Navy there was no very intimate place for us to meet up again.

That night I told Sam that if wanted to see me again he should come to the library. From the library he could walk me home. That was the extent of our relationship for several months.

My parents provided money for books and for the boarding house, but I had to work during college for all my other expenses. I worked as a waitress at a fountain at the drugstore.

I was a terrible waitress and didn't know how to make anything; they had to teach me and at times, one time in particular, I got it wrong anyway.

One day my new boyfriend Sam came to the soda fountain and wanted a malt to drink. In making the malt I gave him an extra scoop of ice cream, so they fired me.

After that I found work that suited me better. My next job involved working with a handicapped young woman student, helping her in school and reading to her.

Then I got another job organizing and typing a thesis for a student who was semi-blind. She had collected a lot of material so I collated and wrote up the results of her research. After that I had a secretarial job for an instructor.

Meanwhile Sam was introducing me to more of the American way of life—cokes and milkshakes and all the rest.

My parents were very different from Sam's but he and they liked each other. My father was impressed that Sam knew about classical music, including the great composers, and they had lively discussions about the relative merits of Beethoven and Brahms and the like.

But as our romance continued World War II started and Sam was sent to midshipman school in Chicago. I interrupted my schooling at that point and instead took a job with Southern Pacific scheduling trains for servicemen.

One Sunday the phone rang and it was Sam. He said, "Come to Chicago and let's get married!"

But my parents insisted that we marry in the Bay Area, not Chicago. We were married in April of 1945. We had to wait until Sam graduated from Midshipman School.

Meanwhile Sam's parents were insisting that we be married in a Jewish temple. The problem with that was that it was *Pesach*, so the food for the wedding had to be specially prepared. But we worked it out so that we were married in a temple.

I was 19 when we married and Sam was 20, and neither of us had a car.

My dad had loaned us his car so we could drive to Carmel, California after the wedding. From Carmel we took a train to Chicago, where we attended a concert as part of our honeymoon.

After that we made our way to Bainbridge, Maryland, and from there, to Miami where Sam would have small ship duty for the next three or four months.

It reminded me in a way of my past life spent on the go. But now I was happy—very happy—in a way I could not have imagined back then.

CHAPTER THIRTY

MARRIED LIFE

Our brief time in Miami before Sam was sent overseas to the Philippines during the war was perhaps the happiest of my life; it was definitely the most carefree.

For our living quarters Sam and I had a little cottage to ourselves of the kind provided for officers. Sam worked very hard from 7 A.M. to 7 P.M., but meanwhile I had the days to myself. It was leisure of a sort I could scarcely have imagined.

Life was not as carefree for Sam who was still working hard in small ship school and facing deployment, possibly to someplace dangerous since the war was still on. But we made the best of things.

In the evenings we would go out to dinner and see a movie. For recreation there was a huge Olympic sized pool on the base and we had access to sailboats, bicycles, and other recreational vehicles. I would often go to the library, swim in the pool, or visit with the other wives. Sometimes I rented a bicycle and bicycled around Miami on my own. There was maid service in our little cottage so I had no worries about cleaning. It was the most fabulous time, at least for me!

Meanwhile Sam's work on base and the things he was learning were completely secret. And since I had time to myself to imagine all kinds of things, I sometimes wondered if he thought I might be a German spy, thus his extreme secrecy! But while that was not the case, he never to this day has told me anything about his small ship training in Miami.

From those times I also remember the tall beautiful coconut palms of Miami, and Sam and me knocking two or three of the big hairy brown coconuts down from a palm tree, cracking them open and drinking their delicious milk.

Sam was still just 20 then, and he would get his pay, a small amount but enough to live on with all the free extras provided on base. Sam kept the money in a shoebox since he didn't want to put it in the bank. Keeping money in a shoebox struck me as hilarious, like we weren't really grownups. My father would have put the money in the bank but Sam felt differently.

Everything on base was very cheap. One time Sam bought two boxes of Hershey chocolate bars and we ate those for breakfast, something that would have horrified my German parents. The freedom I felt was probably more delicious than the candy bars!

Sometimes we would sail on the bay, as Sam had learned to do in the Navy. I wrote my parents, sister, and cousin about the glories of not having to do anything. To be sure it would have been hard to imagine a more different life than the one we had lived not all that long ago in Europe.

But after a few months in the paradise of Miami, Sam had to ship out overseas. I moved to New York from there and stayed with my mother's brother, my Uncle Ernst who owned two apartment houses in New York City. I was there for two or three months until the war ended.

Meanwhile Sam was in the Philippines where he stayed for another nine months after the war ended. Once the war was over Sam asked me to move back to San Francisco, since he thought he would be shipped back there earlier than he indeed was.

So I moved back to San Francisco and in with my parents, an adjustment for me again after being away from home so long and so happily. Waiting for Sam's return home, I worked in a jewelry store.

Life in San Francisco after the war was a far cry from my idyllic days spent bicycling, sailing, and drinking coconut milk from the palm trees of balmy Miami. For one thing, when Sam arrived home it was very hard for us to find an apartment in San Francisco. Finally we moved to a small place that neither of us liked but that we could afford.

And Sam himself had changed during his time in the Philippines, where he had run his own ship and gone from being a boy to a man. Now he was harder to please in ways I hadn't experienced or anticipated. For instance, by the time he arrived back in San Francisco he was tired of steak, which he'd always liked before but that had been all they had served on the ship back to the United States.

Other things proved difficult as well for daily living. Sam found it hard to find civilian clothes. We needed a car, and that too was hard to come by. And Sam was not certain what he wanted to do next with his life.

My father wanted Sam to go into the jewelry business with him, but knowing them both, I opposed that idea. I wanted Sam to go to optometry school, but he didn't want to go back to school at all.

Sam returned to Berkeley and eventually did attend optometry school; but these remained hard times for us financially and otherwise. The G.I. Bill paid just 90 dollars a month. For the first time we had trouble getting along, and he had he trouble getting along with my parents.

In 1947 our son Michael was born. It was a difficult birth that left me internally injured and very exhausted. We moved into student housing in UC Berkeley that year and Sam painted the Berkeley stadium for extra money. Our hard times continued. We lived on the third floor of an apartment house for married students. We had no money or furniture. We bought a used crib for the baby.

Eventually Sam graduated from optometry school and my father helped him find a job. Still we continued to have a rough time in those years when Sam was just starting his profession. He felt resentful of my attention to Michael, and I was still having health problems because of Michael's difficult birth. Michael however was a delight, always happy and smiling, the one joy in our lives.

Sam was still working as an optometrist in Oakland when he met another optometrist who told him about a practice in Los Angeles. So we moved to Los Angeles and from that point things got better for us. I loved Los Angeles right from the start. I have always loved the ocean and today we live in Santa Monica overlooking the ocean. There is no nicer place than Santa Monica. Every day I look at the ocean.

CHAPTER THIRTY-ONE

BEING AMERICAN

Michael was born in 1947 when we were still in the Bay Area and our daughter Barbara was born in 1950 in Los Angeles. Our children's lives growing up in Southern California in the 1950's were much different from mine growing up in Germany.

Everything in California and the United States generally is more open and relaxed than in Germany. And in Germany when I was a child, even children's toys were geared toward turning children into adults. In America kids are allowed to just be kids and have fun.

In Germany children of my generation had very little freedom. I had a lot of responsibilities, after Hitler came to power. I had to grow up very fast even before age six, and an awful lot of discipline was imposed on me from a very young age. Being a kid in Germany was much more restricted than being a kid in America. Children in Germany when I was growing up had no choices but lots of supervision. Everything was planned out for children who then had to follow the plan.

Although I would not ever trade any part of my American life for the one I had or would have had in Germany, I do feel that a lot of people in the United States today lack the sort of discipline and capacity for delayed gratification taught to European children. Among the children I knew as a child in Germany, a small segment to be sure, I recall that we were more disciplined and that more was expected of us than of American children the same age. We had better manners and more respect for adults, and we were taught to be less demanding of adult attention and material things.

However, that said, I did not treat my children the way I was treated as a child because I thought it was harmful. I think it destroys a child's creativity. I was neither a typical German mom nor a typical American mom, but perhaps something in between.

But now that my children are adults I can also say that I am more self-confident than either; and I believe that this comes from my harsher German childhood. So while I would not have wished my childhood on anyone, least of all my own children, it did give me certain abilities to cope that served me well later on.

❀

In our first years in Los Angeles before Barbara was born, we lived in an apartment building. A woman took care of Michael when I worked in Sam's office as his receptionist. After eight or nine months he hired a regular receptionist and I stayed home with Michael.

I liked working at Sam's office for those first several months though, and learning about his practice. At lunch I would go downtown, an interesting area and a much cleaner, safer one than downtown L.A. today. Back then I enjoyed shopping at the Broadway department store and other similar stores. Then after work Sam and I would have dinner out together and then we would drive home to Michael.

The people downstairs from where we lived had an angry little boy who bullied Michael whenever he came outside to play, so we had to move. We moved to a ground floor apartment, which was better for Michael. There he could play and was happy, and I no longer had to be worried about him.

After I became pregnant with Barbara we moved to a duplex in Beverly Hills. Barbara was born in Beverly Hills, and shortly after that the Korean War started. Sam did not sign up for the reserves but I was apprehensive nevertheless about his being called back into the Navy. That never happened, although we did have some other challenges.

One day Sam woke up severely nauseated and was unable to drive to work. As it turned out he had an ear infection, but he couldn't drive for two weeks. By then we had two kids, and he also had two offices to maintain. So I had to drive him around to both offices until he could drive himself again.

We also had some good luck around then. One day an optometrist friend of Sam's loaned him money to buy a house. Barbara was two; Michael was five. Our first house was in Studio City off of Laurel Canyon on a cul-de-sac. The house was all redwood inside and out. It had a large living room/dining room combination, divided by a beautiful hallway. We also had a brick fireplace downstairs. All the bedrooms were upstairs, a master bedroom for Sam and me and bedrooms for Barbara and Michael.

Our downstairs kitchen was on the same level as the living room/dining room and contained a brick wall with a built in oven. We also had an outside barbecue and a lovely large back yard. Our kids played with all the neighbors' children, rode bicycles, and had fun together. They all took a school bus to school.

This was a very nice time for Sam and me. Sam's practice was flourishing. He opened another practice with a partner in North Hollywood. We became comfortable financially. Eventually we did some landscaping which turned out very beautiful and then we put in a swimming pool. I spent most of my time with the children and their activities but even then I was yearning for something more, some more challenging way to use my mind although I didn't know exactly what.

Michael was in Little League and took cello lessons and Barbara was in Campfire Girls. She also took piano and drawing lessons. She went to a little art school near us. Everything was good for us, and life was the most relaxed and comfortable I had ever known. I was experiencing all the good things America had to offer.

We began to feel we needed more space so we bought another house, not too far away so the kids could continue in the same school. Sam joined a quartet and played violin. We had several recitals in our home. We invited friends and the children played in the recitals. And we had lots of friends, parties, in general a very pleasant time. It was a nice San Fernando Valley kind of existence, and very different from either the stresses of my girlhood or the insecurity of my San Francisco days.

After graduating from high school Michael went to San Francisco State University at first and later transferred to UC Berkeley. Barbara attended UCLA. Both of our children were close to my parents, and Michael in particular visited them often while at college in the Bay Area.

❖

My own relationship with my parents remained ambiguous. While pleased that Sam and I were doing well, they found our second house too ostentatious for their European taste. They were still living in San Francisco, and they still had a picture in their minds of Sam and me as struggling kids who still lived in student housing and could not even afford a new crib for Michael. So when they first saw our beautiful home and garden, and that we were able to live comfortably, they had trouble visualizing us as adults who had become successful.

And they were getting old. Our success may have seemed bittersweet to them after everything that they had had to give up.

CHAPTER THIRTY-TWO

A NEW PROFESSION

Once Michael was away at college and Barbara was a teenager I found myself with some free time. One day I saw an ad for law school in the newspaper and that they were offering classes not far from where we lived. I said to myself that this was something I would like to do. My childhood dream of studying law had never left me but, as I now realized, it had been put on hold for a very long time.

So I drove to the location that was advertised, an office building. The law school was on the fourth floor. The receptionist there gave me an application. While there I met another woman who was applying who had researched the school, the San Fernando Valley College of Law. She told me the school was legitimate and that she knew someone who had taken the bar and passed. So I enrolled.

Right away I loved law school. After deferring my childhood dream for so long, attending law school made me feel as if I had been reborn.

Still it wasn't easy attending law school as a woman or an older student; and as I found, the biggest challenges were non-academic ones.

Nowadays no one would probably think twice about a married woman in her late thirties attending law school after her children were grown, but back then it was considered a very unusual thing to do. Many I knew, including some good friends disapproved.

My own mother was among those who felt resentful that I had decided to attend law school and become an attorney. My guess is that my newfound vocation, especially in middle age, may have reawakened some of her own, long-buried frustrations and disappointments.

As a young woman in Germany my mother had been pushed into roles as a housewife and mother that she had never really liked; but in that time and place women had had fewer choices, far fewer in fact, than I did in my youth.

So my mother coped but never flourished as I was able to do—an example not just of how far women have come in this century and the last, but also of the steep price immigrants pay for their children's future happiness.

Once we were settled in America my mother still played tennis and later my parents played golf. But my mother never drove a car, and metaphorically speaking, never steered her own life. I would like to think that my being able to finally realize my dream of being a lawyer and judge gave her some satisfaction, even vicarious satisfaction, but I am not sure.

I commuted to and from law school, a 25 minute commute each way. Meanwhile I still had a house to maintain, a teenage daughter at home, a dog, a cat, and all my other old responsibilities. So I studied around those things, from 3 A.M. to 6:30 A.M. every day.

I lost all my friends except for one, and although I made new ones, it hurt to lose those friends.

My greatest source of support through all this was Sam. He only regretted that I couldn't play golf with him anymore. Michael was busy with school. Barbara on the other hand did feel unhappy since she was still at home and no other mothers she knew went to law school then. But those were what the times were like back then, and they presented some challenges women likely would not face today, or at least would not face in the same way.

Still, I never felt better within myself than when I made up my mind to pursue my dream.

CHAPTER THIRTY-THREE

PRACTICING LAW AND BEYOND

Once I graduated from law school and passed the bar I worked at first for a general law firm in Beverly Hills. Then one day I saw an ad in the paper for a position with the Department of Real Estate in downtown Los Angeles. After applying for and securing that job I worked there for five years practicing real estate law. I then transferred to Department of Industrial Relations for the State of California.

With that experience, I opened my own law office. After about a year and a half of that, I met a judge from the Workers' Compensation Appeals Board who encouraged me to apply to become a judge there.

Along with my dream of practicing law I had always dreamed of being a judge; now it seemed that the second part of my long cherished wish might come true! So I applied for the job, passed an exam, and was appointed a Workers Compensation Appeals Board judge, a job I held for over 15 years.

By then I was 68 years old and Sam had retired from his practice. He wanted some company in his retirement, so I retired.

Although I still loved the work, I was also facing some challenges about then that made the idea of retirement more appealing. For example I had an overload of cases, no secretary, and due to funding cuts less and less office support in general.

Sam was at a point of wanting to travel and do other things we'd not yet done, so we made a mutual decision that I would retire. It was a good decision, and we have had a lot of fun since then traveling, reading, enjoying music, playing bridge, and spending time with our children, grandchildren, and other relatives and friends. Life has been especially good to us in our later years.

Looking back I can say I have been able to "have it all", although not without cost.

❖

Once we were all here in America, to their credit neither my mother nor my Aunt Ilse, her sister, ever complained or looked back. My Uncle Erwin went back to Germany several times and vacationed there, although my father never did.

Cousin Walter became a certified public accountant (CPA) and was very successful. He married a woman from Sweden who is a nurse. Today they live in British Columbia. Cousin Anne lives in Seattle with her husband. They have four children. Anne became a psychologist and also belongs to a support group for children of German refugees.

My sister Susi lives in Southern California.

My parents lived the rest of their lives in San Francisco.

And Sam and I still live in Santa Monica—a melting pot of cultures that overlooks the vast Pacific where my immigrant soul has found a home.

Made in the USA
San Bernardino, CA
12 August 2020